*Grieving the Loss of
Someone You Love*

Parker,

This little book contains big wisdom. Pick and choose the parts you want to read – or read it straight through. Know that you are loved.

Love in Him,
Patty + Peter Wonderly

Grieving the Loss of Someone You Love

Daily Meditations to Help You through the Grieving Process

Raymond R. Mitsch
and
Lynn Brookside

Servant Publications
Ann Arbor, Michigan

Vine Books is an imprint of Servant Publications especially
designed to serve Evangelical Christians.

Scripture texts used in this work, unless otherwise indicated,
are from the New International Version, copyright © 1978,
by New York International Bible Society, published by the
B.B. Kirkbride Bible Company, Inc. (Indianapolis, Indiana)
and The Zondervan Corporation (Grand Rapids, Michigan).
Those marked (TLB) are from The Living Bible, copyright
© 1971, Tyndale House Publishers, Wheaton, IL.

While every effort has been made to trace copyright holders,
if there should be any error or omission, the publishers will
be happy to rectify this at the first opportunity.

Published by Servant Publications
P.O. Box 8617
Ann Arbor, Michigan 48107

Cover design by Gerald L. Gawronski/The Look Design

00 01 02 03 15 14

Printed in the United States of America
ISBN 0-89283-822-1

Library of Congress Cataloging-in-Publication Data

Mitsch, Ray.
    Grieving the loss of someone you love : daily meditations
to help you through the grieving process / Raymond R.
Mitsch and Lynn Brookside.
        p. cm.
    ISBN 0-89283-822-1
    1. Grief—Religious aspects—Christianity—Meditations.
2. Consolation—Meditations. I. Brookside, Lynn. II. Title.
BV4905.2.M56 1993
242'.4—dc20   93-29618

Contents

Introduction

R AY went out on an emergency call a couple of years ago with his father-in-law, Paul, who is a veterinarian. Paul had been called to his animal clinic because a dog had been badly injured in a car accident. Once he had determined that the pooch was too injured to be helped there was nothing left to do but put him out of his misery. Ray assisted Paul by holding the frightened dog in his arms while Paul gave the dog a fatal dose of a sleep-inducing drug. Ray was stunned by the remarkable swiftness with which the animal moved from life to death. In an instant, a living, breathing being was gone, never to return. Ray was compelled to face, once more, how fragile life is. The entire experience brought back all of his grief over his father's death.

Ray's dad died when he was just twelve years old. An only child, Ray and his dad had been extremely close. His dad's death came at a time in Ray's life when he was particularly vulnerable to feelings of loss and isolation. In addition, adolescents and pre-adolescents are particularly keen on having control over their lives, so the powerlessness Ray felt in the face of death was even more devastating than it might otherwise have been.

Ray was too young to have the resources to grieve adequately. He was afraid to cry for fear of appearing to be a sissy. He was unaware of the havoc that unexpressed grief can play in a person's life, so he had a much greater incentive—or so he thought—for stuffing down his sorrow and "getting on with his life" than he did for expressing his sorrow. Besides, Ray's mother was counting on him to be "the man of the family" now. He had to be strong for her.

All these things caused Ray to postpone dealing with his sorrow. Now, years later, Ray finds that he's forced to deal with his grief a little at a time as opportunities like putting down a dog present themselves. Perhaps that's one reason Ray has chosen to become a psychologist, so that he can help others avoid the pitfalls into which he fell. That's certainly why he wanted to write this book.

Lynn had a similar experience. When Lynn lost her first child within hours after her birth she didn't know how to grieve. She hid her sorrow deep within and vowed never to let it out. It took many years for her to come to a place where she felt able to release her immense sadness. During those years her hidden grief took its toll. It was only when she finally acknowledged and processed her grief that she was able to shake off its effects.

Our hope is that you, the reader, will experience "good grief." That you will use the pages of this book as signposts meant to lead you to the other side of your grief.

The psychic wound we experience when we lose a

loved one to death is much like the physical wound caused by a bad burn. Burn victims are in extreme danger of infection. If an infection takes hold under the scab that develops over the burn it can become life-threatening, even when the burn itself is not. The only way to be sure that no infection develops is to scrub the wound periodically, which is extremely painful and said to be one of the worst aspects of the healing process.

Unfortunately, the choices we face as people who are grieving are not so clear-cut. Many of us opt to take what looks like the easy way out. Once the memorial service is over some of us refuse to continue to "scrub" the wound caused by our loss, declining to deal with the "infection" that may be developing just below the surface. We are either unaware of, or unwilling to face, the emotional death that may lie in our future as a result of this neglect.

Until recently, more serious burns, those that covered a large portion of the body, presented an even greater risk. Burns tend to ooze liquid from the lymphatic system. People often say that the burn is "weeping" because droplets of liquid seep from the wound. Before the advent of synthetic skin people were known to die from losing too many precious bodily fluids before skin grafts could be done. In many ways, the grieving process parallels this problem, for it's possible to keep our wound open too long, to get "stuck" in our grief, and to allow it to drain energy and the very life from us.

In our culture we tend to acknowledge physical

wounds but neglect emotional ones. That's particularly true where grief is concerned. We would not expect a burn victim to show up at work after only three or four days in the hospital on the theory that he will "work" himself back to health. Yet, traditionally, employers in this country allow for only three or four days of bereavement leave. For some reason we seem to expect people to "work" their way out of their grief. It was not always so.

There was a time, not so many generations ago, when people routinely expected a family to "go into mourning" for a year or more after the death of someone close. It was traditional for people to wear black for an entire year following the death of a loved one. Wearing black was more than just a formality. It was a way of reminding themselves and those around them that they were still in a fragile state and needed to be treated with special regard.

The grieving process is never "neat and clean." It wasn't so generations ago and it isn't today. There is nothing pleasant about experiencing that kind of sorrow. It is intensely painful, even gut-wrenching, and it takes time; often, lots of time. In the process we may ask questions we have never asked before, questions about the nature of God and the worth of life in general. We feel numb. We feel confused. At times, we may feel enraged. But most of all, we feel the hurt.

There is no standard for grieving. Loss affects each of us differently so, of course, people don't grieve exactly the same. In spite of all our differences, however, there are still some constants in the way humans deal with grief. It is these constants that we have addressed in this book.

We are aware that our readers will be at different stages of grief. Some will have lost their loved one only recently. Others may have suffered their loss some time ago. We have endeavored to minister to the needs of people in both groups. Your pain is real regardless of how long ago you lost your loved one.

Because we each move through grief in our own way, at our own pace, the devotionals contained here are not necessarily meant to be read in order. You may find that one is more fitting for a particular day than another. You may decide to go back to one that seems more suited to your needs on a certain day. Or you may wish to jump ahead in search of something that will speak to your needs on this day or that. That's okay. This book is merely meant to be a tool. The important thing is to keep scrubbing your wound. Eventually, in God's time, your tears will turn to laughter and your mourning into dancing.

Ray Mitsch, Ph.D.
Geneva, Illinois

Lynn Brookside
Escondido, California

1 Even Christians Grieve

Brothers, we do not want you to be ignorant about those who fall asleep, or to grieve like the rest of men, who have no hope. We believe that Jesus died and rose again and so we believe that God will bring with Jesus those who have fallen asleep in him. According to the Lord's own word, we tell you that we who are still alive, who are left till the coming of the Lord, will certainly not precede those who have fallen asleep. For the Lord himself will come down from heaven, with a loud command, with the voice of the archangel and the trumpet call of God, and the dead in Christ will rise first. After that, we who are still alive and are left will be caught up with them in the clouds to meet the Lord in the air. And so we will be with the Lord forever. Therefore encourage each other with these words.

1 Thessalonians 4:13-18

A FRIEND of Lynn's, Kate Dunbar, tells this story about attending a seminar given by psychiatrist and author Elisabeth Kubler-Ross: "I sat listening to this tiny dynamo describing in her heavily accented English an incident that occurred while she was doing the research she later published in *On Death and Dying*. Kubler-Ross visited an extremely large hospital in search of terminal patients willing to speak with her about their experiences with death and dying. She said that by the time she had worked her way from the first floor to the twenty-second, she had not located one doctor or a single nurse who was willing to admit that any of their patients was terminal. In the entire hospital there was not one patient dying! Yet, there was a morgue in the basement that ran the entire length of the building. 'That,' Kubler-Ross said, 'Was when I realized that I *must* educate!'"

Since that time, Kubler-Ross has forever changed our culture's attitude toward death and dying. Through her research she has identified the five stages of grief, providing a road map, of sorts, for all who must traverse that hitherto unknown territory. It is true, of course, that each of us grieves somewhat differently. Each of us is an individual, so naturally we grieve as individuals. There is no one road map that is perfectly suited to everyone, but there are certain major landmarks most of us will pass on our path to healing.

According to Kubler-Ross those landmarks, or stages, of grief are: denial, anger, bargaining, sorrow and acceptance. We will not necessarily feel all of those things in that particular order. In fact, we probably will not. But those reactions will appear from time to time throughout our grieving process. At times they will be mixed together, one feeling piled on another. We may find ourselves angry, bargaining and denying all at the same time, or in quick succession. At other times we may find ourselves deeply mired in one particular stage for a matter of weeks or, in some cases, months. One thing is nearly certain, however, we will pass through all of those stages sometime during our grieving process —even if we are Christians.

Christians are not exempt from grief, not yet anyway. When we lose someone, we, too, will deny; we will hurt; we will weep; we will rage; we may even bargain with God. The difference for us is that we have *hope*. We have the hope of one day seeing our loved ones again and the comfort of knowing that we do not walk alone through the storm of grief. We are members of a family—the family of God. We can take our denial, our rage, our desire to bargain and our sadness to our loving heavenly Father, who can and will carve stepping stones of them—stepping stones leading to acceptance and, ultimately, healing.

If we trust in him, all things are possible, including, or especially, our healing. Trust him for that when you can and forgive yourself when your pain makes it so that you cannot. God is faithful and true, a rock upon which you can base your faith, even as the wind howls around you.

2 | Help through the Grief

---

*Carry each other's burdens, and in this
way you will fulfill the law of Christ.*

Galatians 6:2

HEN we first receive the news
that someone we love has died,
most of us experience some degree of shock. Shock is a
normal, God-given response to this sort of traumatic
news. It sees us through the first difficult days immediately following our loss. It gives us time to process the
gravity of that loss and allows us to "wake up" to its
true import gradually.

Eventually, however, the shock wears off and we are
faced with the painful reality of our loss. It is then that
we truly need our friends and family to be there for us.
Too often, however, our friends come near only during
the first few days following the death of our loved one.
Then they gradually drift back to their own lives, most
of them convinced that we are functioning quite well
without their help. They have seen us maneuver through
those first few days while our pain is still numbed by

our shock. They don't desert us deliberately; they actually believe we have no particular need of them. And we live in such a fast paced, overloaded-with-responsibilities society that the everyday demands of their schedules can squeeze out even the best intentions to keep in touch, to offer assistance. Only those who have lost a loved one may be aware that we are really heading into the center of the storm rather than coming out of it.

It's important for us to give ourselves permission to ask people to meet our need for comfort so they know that need is legitimate. We need not feel apologetic. We can take it upon ourselves to remind close friends and family members that we are still in the midst of the storm. Those reminders don't have to be confrontational. We can simply tell our friends that we are having a particularly difficult day, that we are missing our loved one a great deal just now. And we can ask them to help us through our grief. Most people we are close to will respond to such a reminder. They need only to be invited to deal with our hurt. Naturally, we all have some friends or family members who have difficulty dealing with people on an emotional level. Those are not the ones to turn to for comfort. But most of us have at least one person in our lives who will respond in love when we make our needs clear to them. We need not walk through this storm alone.

It's also important to be mindful of the fact that Christ is always beside us, walking with us through the storm. But we mustn't fall into the trap of believing that our awareness of Christ's closeness is all we need.

That is simply not so. God created us to be in fellowship with others of our kind. We are not being immature Christians, "disloyal" to God, or ungrateful when we openly acknowledge that we need to be comforted by friends and family.

Make it a goal today to reach out to someone and be honest with them about the space you occupy, just now, within the storm.

3 | *Going Crazy*

*I'm past the point of going
   quietly insane.
I'm getting quite
   noisy about it.
The neighbors must think
   I'm mad.
The neighbors, for once,
   think right.*

Peter McWilliams
How to Survive the Loss of a Love

 *I*T is not unusual for people to report that they feel as if they are "going crazy" following the death of a loved one. When they describe the symptoms of their "craziness" it becomes apparent that they are describing the symptoms of intense stress and anxiety.

Many people report short-term memory loss, which is often a symptom of high anxiety. The mind is paralyzed and overloaded. Loss of memory is annoying but it will pass. It will pass far more quickly if you go easy on yourself and accept this temporary manifestation of your grief.

People also report a re-living of the last time they saw their loved one alive. Ray still occasionally flashes back to his last visit with his dad. That memory is so vivid, he almost feels as if he is there with his dad again. He remembers the feeling of sitting on the window ledge in the hospital room. He remembers what the ball field looked like outside the window. He recalls the conversation he had with his dad about "nothing in particular."

Others report a loss of concentration. Their racing thoughts seem to swirl in their minds in no pattern, to no purpose. They can't think anything through to a conclusion. On the other hand, some report a slowing of their thoughts, or a kind of clouded consciousness, as if they are moving through a mist. They can't focus; nothing seems quite real. All of these symptoms are perfectly ordinary considering the intensity of the sorrow being endured.

Still others report symptoms that would suggest panic attacks, a fight or flight response: increased heart rate, speeding of respiration, cotton mouth, profuse perspiring. Unlike panic attacks, however, these symptoms are brought on by an identifiable event and are likely to disappear as people move through their grief.

Some develop physical symptoms that mimic other ailments. For example, people may believe that they are having a heart attack, with all the attendant symptoms, or migraines, or they develop the habit of grinding their teeth.

Still others seem as if they have developed the symptoms of depression. And although the symptoms of depression—intense sadness, feelings of helplessness, hopelessness and powerlessness—are the same as many of the symptoms of grief, there is a difference. Grief is a natural process that comes to an end without intervention. Depression generally requires professional intervention in order to alleviate it. Depression may develop if a person tries to bypass the grieving process, but the process, itself, is not depression.

If you have found yourself experiencing any of these symptoms, take heart. They will pass. Naturally, it is wise to have a doctor look into any alarming physical symptoms, but chances are those symptoms will disappear in time—if you are faithful about processing your grief.

The symptoms we manifest during this time of crisis are actually a sign of the wondrous way God created human beings. Our minds and bodies are designed to declare a sort of "red alert" that is meant to force us to slow down and pay attention to our needs.

So, if possible, be grateful for the way God has provided for every eventuality in your life and try to slow down. Remember, go easy on yourself. This too shall pass.

4 *In the Beginning*

> *If only my anguish could be weighed and all my misery be placed on the scales! It would surely outweigh the sand of the seas.*
>
> **Job 6:2-3**

I N the beginning, when our grief is brand new, we may find ourselves inconsolable, unable to receive the well-meant and, often, scripturally accurate words of encouragement offered by our Christian friends. When we fail to be comforted by God's Word we may fear it has lost its power for us. Usually, this is not the case. When we have experienced the shock of a major loss, sometimes our minds go into neutral. We find comfort in absolutely nothing and are too distracted to concentrate on the Scriptures. Our questions and doubts make it impossible to pray. We may even feel that God is either unwilling or unable to relieve our pain. Rest assured, God is not ashamed to claim us as his children even when our pain causes us to doubt him or his intentions toward us.

Some of us even rage inside when well-meaning friends quote Scripture in an effort to provide a point of stability in our storm of grief. We don't want to hear comforting words just now. It feels as if their efforts to comfort merely mock us. We feel as if we are beyond comfort. We may think to ourselves, *Can't they see that my pain is real? Do these people think my wound is so insignificant that their feeble attempts to provide comfort will actually ease my pain?*

If you've responded in this way and are feeling guilty, it may help to know that your response is not uncommon. Many have walked this road ahead of you. Many have felt the same and have entertained the same questions. Even Job, acknowledged by God as a righteous man, wanted to know where God was while he was grieving. Job wanted to know what God was doing that was so much more important than relieving him of his distress.

When we are in this early stage of grief, unable to find comfort in anything, it can be immensely helpful to know that this stage will pass. It may not feel as if it will, but it will. There will come a day, in the not too distant future, when you will be able to concentrate once more. You will be able to think clearly. You will, once again, grasp the meanings of the Scriptures you read. Until then, try to get as much rest as possible and go easy on yourself. Don't expect to accomplish much. You can "retire" from the world for this short time without guilt. You are not being lazy. You are simply acknowledging the depth of your loss and your human need for time to recover.

If you need to, declare yourself to be "off duty" today. Postpone anything that can wait until a day when you are feeling more energetic. That day will come... in God's time.

5 | Just Tell Me the Rules

Those who live the abundant life seem to seize each experience, tragic or joyous, and squeeze every drop of learning out of it into their cup of life. Some of us are envious of the... quality of their life-style. But we have forgotten what price that kind of honesty and courage has cost. Joyce Landorf

Mourning Song

*O*UR lives are made up of "rules." Unconsciously, we follow hundreds of rules every day. Most of us follow a prescribed routine for brushing our teeth, for making our morning coffee, for driving in traffic. We have learned rules to help us cope with hundreds of everyday occurrences.

When we are confronted by the loss of a loved one, it is only natural that we should go looking for "rules" to help us cope. Unfortunately, few of us are ever taught how to grieve. Isn't it strange that in a world where loss is inevitable, no one teaches a course on grieving? To be sure, such a course would vary drastically from country to country, and, seemingly, the people in some cultures are better at modeling appropriate grieving behavior than we Americans. But we rarely ever encounter anyone who is able to tell us how to go about grieving. Grief seems to happen *to* us rather than happen with our assent.

Ray's mom sent him to stay with a family friend, Gloria, immediately following his dad's death. Gloria returned him to his mom at the funeral a few days later. During the drive to the funeral, Gloria attempted to instruct Ray on appropriate ways to receive condolences from people. It was a tender attempt on her part to prepare a terrified twelve-year-old boy for what was to come, but it was not an effort to teach Ray how to grieve for himself. It was an attempt to teach him how to help others deal with their grief.

Too often in this country it is the people who feel the loss most keenly who are given—or who assume— the responsibility for making everyone else feel better. Does this sound rational? It doesn't to us. Perhaps we need to step back and honestly assess most of our assumptions in regard to grieving. We need to examine what we expect of ourselves as well as what others seem to expect of us.

When we perceive that a tradition will be detrimental to our emotional well-being, we need to give ourselves permission to break with tradition. The only "rules" we really need to pay attention to are the ones presented to us in the Scriptures. So, if we feel the need to weep openly in a public place, but our sense of propriety tells us we must not, we need to step back and examine that prohibition. Are we worried about what others will think? Perhaps what they will think is, "I know just how he (or she) feels. I felt the same way when I lost my loved one. I wish I had had the guts to weep openly like that. Maybe then I would have healed more readily."

Following the death of his beloved wife, C.S. Lewis noticed people deciding whether or not to mention his loss as they approached him. He said that he hated it when they did mention it and he hated it when they didn't. That is the predicament many people find themselves in when they come upon us after the death of someone we love. It will ease things for everyone if we can acknowledge the awkwardness people may feel and give them permission to respond as best they can. It will also free us to be ourselves, acknowledging the full force of our feelings.

Of course there are people who are uncomfortable with any hint of emotion. Not everyone handles emotional expressiveness well. If we choose to express our feelings openly, then we will also need to be accepting of others who indicate to us that they are disturbed by it. Their distress should never prevent us from continuing to express our sorrow honestly, but it may lead us to be selective about those with whom we choose to be so expressive in the future.

The point is that we will be healthier and more realistic if we do not simply assume that everyone in our world is so fragile that we dare not "burden" them with our true feelings. Let them tell us if they are distressed by our sorrow. Perhaps we will be teaching a mini-course on grieving, helping others to learn to face their experiences, both the tragic and the joyous, with honesty and courage.

Today, vow to be "real" with your friends and family, and be accepting of the ways in which people handle your reality. Truly, there is nothing to lose and so much to be gained.

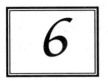

6 Define "Normal"

> *Teach me how to know death*
> *and go on with life.*
> *Teach me how to love life*
> *and not fear death.*   Judith Viorst
>
> *Necessary Losses*

MOST people who are confronted with a new experience want to know what is "normal," or what to expect as a result of that new experience. This is true whether the result is one of grieving or one of happiness.

It might seem unnecessary to tell someone in the midst of grief what it feels like to grieve but it is not really as outlandish as it seems. It can be immensely helpful to know that what we are experiencing is normal for someone who has suffered a loss. So, what is likely to be a part of this experience we call grieving? There are feelings of immense sadness, helplessness, hopelessness, fear, emptiness, irritability, anger, guilt, restlessness and isolation. We may experience a change in appetite, sleep patterns or sex drive. And we can expect to spend some time feeling enormous fatigue. We may even experience clumsiness for a period of time or a lack of concentration and motivation.

All of these symptoms fall well within the range of "normal" for anyone who has experienced a loss and will be far less disconcerting if planned for. Please do not misunderstand, we are not suggesting that you need to plan to go into a blue funk for a specific period of time or that you should pencil in "hopelessness" on your calendar. That's not what we mean when we suggest that you plan for these things to occur. It is very likely, however, that most of these feelings and reactions will be part of your grief experience. You will heal more quickly and fully if you accept all of these facets of grief as part of your healing process.

Especially during the first several weeks following your loss, plan to get more rest than usual. The emotional wound resulting from such a great loss actually requires physical energy to heal, so if you seem to need more sleep right now, be accepting of that fact. Insomnia is not unusual in the early stages of grief and you may want to consult a physician if you are experiencing insomnia, but remember, just sitting or lying in bed can be restful too. Later, once the initial "red alert" declared by your mind and body has subsided, productive work can be restful too. It can provide you with a focus outside yourself giving you the opportunity to rest your overtaxed emotions. Be careful not to use work to avoid your pain, but do whatever amount of work seems comfortable and reasonable.

Remember, it takes time to heal—lots of it. Healing is your primary job just now. Be gentle with yourself. You deserve to take whatever length of time is necessary for you to heal fully. Treat yourself with the same care you would offer a close friend if he or she were in a similar situation. The greater your loss, the more time you are going to need to heal. God created humans with a natural ability to heal, so rest assured, healing will happen. In fact, it is happening right now.

7 Warning Signs

> *"For I know the plans I have for you,"*
> *declares the Lord, "plans to prosper you*
> *and not to harm you, plans to give you*
> *hope and a future. Then you will call*
> *upon me and come and pray to me, and I*
> *will listen to you. You will seek me and*
> *find me when you seek me with all your*
> *heart."* Jeremiah 29:11-13

WHILE it can be a great relief to find out that the gut-wrenching feelings of loss and sadness you may be experiencing are "normal," we would be remiss if we did not also warn you about some feelings or signals that are not uncommon but must never be ignored.

With the help of a handful of understanding friends or family members who are willing to listen and pray— both with us and for us—most people can weather their personal storm of grief without professional help. There are times, however, when professional help is necessary. These times are signaled by the following:

thoughts of suicide, feeling as if you are going to fly apart or that you are out of control, feeling completely isolated. You should also seek professional help if you have a history of emotional disturbances, or if you find yourself using drugs (prescription or otherwise) or alcohol in order to deal with your loss. Sedatives, tranquilizers and anti-depressants may interfere with the grief process. It is important never to take any of the above without careful supervision by a doctor who is aware of your loss.

Remember, suicide is never an answer to any problem. It may seem a perfect way to end the pain you are feeling, but it is a very permanent end to a temporary problem. Your pain may feel as if it has become a constant fixture in your life, but, eventually, it *will* dissipate. You can be absolutely sure of that. God's Word assures us that he has a plan for us, a plan to prosper us and not to harm us, a plan to give us hope and a future. Those things may seem impossible right now, but God listens when we pray. In him, all things are possible.

So, if you are entertaining notions of putting an end to your pain permanently, it is time to talk with a professional. If your need is immediate, call your pastor or dial the operator and ask to be put in touch with a suicide hotline. Almost all towns have at least one such hotline. If the operator asks whether this is an emergency tell him or her "Yes!" without hesitation.

If your suicidal thoughts are not placing you in immediate danger, that does not mean you can safely dismiss them. Shoving those thoughts into a dark corner of your mind and ignoring them has a way of increasing their urgency. Like mushrooms, suicidal thoughts grow in the dark. They must be exposed to the light and uprooted, and you may need help to do it. This is one path you should not try to travel alone.

If you have fallen prey to Satan's lie that death is the only way to put an end to your pain, you need to remind yourself over and over—a hundred times a day if necessary—that you are loved by God and by your Christian family, that you are significant, that God has a plan for your life.

Hold fast to God's promises and seek the help you need in order to make it through this grief. Determine to walk through this storm until you come to the other side. Give yourself the opportunity to discover the plans God has for your future.

8 Being Rather than Doing

> *The thing that destroys a good many of us as Christians is our inability to relate to each other in a warm, honest, compassionate sort of way. Even with those to whom I was close, I failed in this endeavor. I was so busy being a "doing" Christian that I'd forgotten what God called me to be.*
>
> James "Frog" Sullivan
> *The Frog Who Never Became a Prince*

*I*T is not at all uncommon for mourners to feel inundated by offers of assistance, particularly in the days immediately following their loss. During those days and weeks we are usually feeling overwhelmed anyway, so the task of sorting out all the offers of help is just one more chore that can send us into overload.

Most of us are also aware that at least some of those offers of assistance are made more from a desire to be polite or to fill an awkward silence than they are out of a genuine intent to help. Sometimes it seems easier just to refuse all offers than it is to discern the genuine offers from those extended out of courtesy. Besides, we know that even genuine offers are sometimes proffered by people who are not able to deliver, people whose own emotional well-being makes it impossible for them to really be there for us. That knowledge further complicates our decision regarding whose offer to accept and whose to refuse, politely but firmly.

Too often, though, our reason for refusing others' offers of assistance is a mistaken notion that a Christian is to be a helper rather than the one who is helped. We have become human *doings* instead of human *beings*. It can become such a habit to invest ourselves in the *acts* of our faith rather than in our faith, that we lose sight of the fact that the Scriptures are filled with references to godly people *waiting* upon the Lord. Too many of us become caught up in the good feelings we get when we help others. We tend to be uncomfortable with our feeling of vulnerability when we accept help from those same people. We don't want to be a bother. Yet Scripture instructs us to "carry *each other's* burdens" (Galatians 6:2). It goes both ways.

We may also wish to refuse offers of help because we do not want to appear to be needy. We don't want to admit that we haven't done the dishes in a week or that laundry is piled waist high in the laundry room. We don't want to admit that we haven't bothered to cook a decent meal for ourselves since heaven-knows-when. We don't want to admit that, much as we love our kids, just now we would gladly swap them for a little time alone, in peace. We don't want people to know just how depressed we really are. We're afraid of seeming incompetent or unloving.

If we are hospitalized with a broken leg we are not so likely to feel ashamed of our need for help. The visibility of our wound somehow makes it "legitimate." What does this imply about our notion of emotional woundedness? Too many of us have the idea, "If it ain't visible, it ain't important."

God created human beings to be multi-faceted, with bodies, minds and feelings. All of these things are inextricably bound together and cannot be separated. If we are in pain it doesn't really matter whether our wound is physical or emotional. It hurts! We need to work to recognize the legitimacy of our emotional pain.

Make up your mind, today, to accept some of those heartfelt offers of assistance. And thank God for giving you supportive, loving friends and family members who are able—and willing—to help when you need it most.

9 | God's Anesthesia

It is one of the mysteries of our nature that a man, all unprepared, can receive a thunder-stroke like that and live. There is but one reasonable explanation of it. The intellect is stunned by the shock and by groping gathers the meaning of the words. The power to realize their full import is mercifully wanting. The mind has a dumb sense of vast loss—that is all. It will take mind and memory months and possibly years to gather the details and thus learn and know the whole extent of the loss.

Samuel Clemens
The Autobiography of Mark Twain

W HEN we experience a great shock, as we do when we lose someone we love, that shock alters our perceptions for a time. Colors seem drab, bird songs seem out of tune —if we hear them at all. Even our favorite foods seem tasteless. The entire world seems out of focus.

Often we feel numb, and any movement is an effort. We may even forget the most common elements of our lives. We may suddenly look around us at a stop sign and realize we have no idea where we are, only to discover, when we really concentrate, that we are mere blocks from our home. Ray's recently bereaved friend stood, staring at someone in utter confusion, unable to remember the telephone number she had called her own for more than nine years.

Such occurrences are common among the bereaved. They can be disconcerting but, if we are careful, they are seldom dangerous. Certainly, if you find yourself terribly distracted and unable to concentrate, it would be an excellent idea to arrange for others to drive you places until you are tracking better. You will want to ask for input from people you trust when making decisions that cannot be postponed. Otherwise, you can simply "sit tight" and wait for this particular phase of your grief to pass. Be assured, it will.

There may be a few people who will interpret your shock as indifference. You may even be confused by it yourself. One woman, Margie, had a difficult time forgiving herself for being "heartless" because the afternoon of the day her mother died she took her daughter shopping for a formal to wear to the prom. Looking back, Margie could not understand why she thought clothes shopping was such an important chore that it could not be postponed. She was ashamed of herself because she had not been consumed by sorrow immediately upon hearing the news of her mother's death.

If you've had a similar experience, there's no need to

feel ashamed. The fact that you functioned so well immediately following the death of your loved one does not, in any way, indicate that you are unloving or unfeeling. It is simply a reflection of the wondrous way God has provided for us to function in times of great sorrow. It may be a short while before you feel the full impact of your loss. Be grateful for that. There will be time enough to feel your pain.

The time of shock is a good time to reaffirm your faith. There may be times in the near future when you will have occasion to doubt God and his goodness. You can blunt the force of those doubts if you use this period of shock to confirm and reestablish your faith in God and in the truth of his Word. Sinking your spiritual roots into the bedrock of God's Word now will allow you to remain rooted and grounded in the midst of the storm.

10 | A Time to Mourn

> *There is a time for everything, and a season for every activity under heaven... a time to weep and a time to laugh, a time to mourn and a time to dance.*
>
> **Ecclesiastes 3:1, 4**

WHEN Lynn was grieving the loss of her first baby she often felt as if she dared not cry for fear she would never stop. It seemed as if there were tears enough within her to fill an ocean. She was afraid people would see her as undisciplined, weak and bothersome, if she allowed herself to express all the grief she felt.

There were times when Lynn saw her grief as a dark and scary place within her mind, a reservoir in which she might dive too deep, never to find her way back to the light at the surface. She was afraid that, if she allowed herself to maneuver within that place of grief, she might reach a "point of no return." So she kept her grief dammed up inside and never went near the reservoir where it was stored.

After many years of holding back her tears, Lynn came to know some loving, knowledgeable people who eventually convinced her that expressing her emotions was not a sign of weakness but of strength. They offered to sit with her in her grief so that she would not need to fear drowning in it. As Lynn began to explore the reservoir within, she discovered that our minds and bodies are created by a loving God who has made provision for all contingencies. He designed us so that our emotions will shut down before we reach the point of no return. We can experience grief only in increments that we can manage. Our bodies can produce only so many tears at one time. We will stop crying before we can do ourselves harm. Our mind will plunge only so far into our reservoir of grief before it brings us back to the surface for a "breather."

It did not happen instantly, but Lynn learned to deal with her grief a little at a time. She learned to share it openly with certain, select friends who had offered to be there for her in her grief. Eventually, she learned that grief lasts only for a season. Finally, she was able to laugh once again.

Are you afraid to "bother" people with your sorrow? Do you fear appearing weak? Quite the opposite is true. It takes great strength to walk through the grief. It takes a commitment to one's self, to those we love and the truth about who God made us to be. Why not commit yourself to finding one person, today, who will sit with you in your grief? Then, face it with courage for a season.

11 | Give Sorrow Words

Give sorrow words: the grief that does not speak
Whispers the o'er fraught heart, and bids it break. **Shakespeare**
Macbeth

SOMETIMES it is not a fear of being overwhelmed that keeps us from expressing our grief with tears. Sometimes it's our anger. Ray felt tremendously angry after his father's death. He was mad at his father for "going off and leaving" him. He was mad at God for taking his father away from him. He was mad at his mother because she couldn't make his pain go away. And he was mad at her for needing him so much because of her own grief. Ray couldn't deal with his sorrow so he translated it into rage.

Many of us are uncomfortable expressing our sorrow because it draws our attention to our need for the comfort others can provide. Anger, on the other hand, allows us to delude ourselves into thinking we don't need anyone. It seems safer not to need anyone, especially when we are still reeling from losing someone we need. We certainly don't want to risk being hurt like that again, so we shut down. Unlike shock, however, this kind of shutting down is not healthful. It keeps us from draining the emotions from our wound.

To complicate matters further, Ray had absorbed our society's view of manhood. Fortunately, that view is changing but in the fifties and sixties men weren't supposed to cry. So at the "manly" age of twelve, Ray bottled up his tears and strove to be a man. He vowed never to let anyone know how deeply he hurt. He spent endless days aching more profoundly than he could have ever imagined possible, yet he determined to keep his pain a secret, even from himself.

Pain doesn't just disappear because we will it to. Unexpressed pain becomes toxic and inevitably takes its toll. It poisons us like a polluted, underground water supply feeding into a spring. Ray's pain leaked into all he did, every decision he made, every moment of his life.

Was it acceptable for you to show your emotions when you were a child? Your answer to that question could provide you with an important clue as to how well you will deal with your grief now. When we rush to get past the tears and get on with our lives we actually short-circuit our healing. There is no quick way to get to the other side of this storm. The only way to the end is through it.

Even our friends and family may tell us to "get over it" and get on with our lives. Doubtless, they are well-intentioned. They hate to see us in pain and wish it to come to a quick end. They are probably unaware that our greatest need is *time* to heal. Pain and grief are uncomfortable but they will not kill us—unless we bottle them up inside. Then they may. Finding no other outlet, that kind of grief will seek its expression in physical ailments that can greatly diminish our quality of life or can, conceivably, result in our ultimate, untimely death.

What greater testimony to the Lord's goodness can we give than to live a full and joyous life even in light of our great loss? In order to do that, however, we need to express our anger appropriately and with God's help face the pain beneath it.

Try to express some of what you feel during your prayer time today. Then, turn and face this new day with hope.

12 Facing Familiar Routines Alone

> I think I am beginning to understand why grief feels like suspense. It comes from the frustration of so many impulses that had become habitual. Thought after thought, feeling after feeling, action after action, had H. as their object. Now their target is gone. I keep on through habit fitting an arrow to the string; then I remember and have to lay the bow down.
>
> **C.S. Lewis**
> *A Grief Observed*

WHETHER we meet our grief with a determined avoidance of tears or a seeming overabundance of them, one thing is sure, our lives have been changed irrevocably. There are times when getting through a day or an hour without stumbling across a reminder of our loved one seems to be our greatest challenge. Even little things—*especially* little things—seem to ambush us, stabbing us with a pang of grief.

For Ray, feeding the family dog after his father's death was one of the most difficult adjustments he had to make. That may sound trivial but it wasn't... not to Ray. Feeding the dog had always been his father's chore and he had performed it faithfully and cheerfully. Now, after all these years, Ray still remembers the feeling of moving through quicksand whenever he prepared the dog's food. His heart was heavy, his mind in a muddle. He was overcome by a feeling of loss. Every move was an effort.

Are there times like that for you? Chores that you must now begin to do? Places you must now go alone?

Lynn's grandmother always missed her deceased husband, a faithful churchgoer, most during her drive to church each Sunday. Her grandparents' Sunday routine was always the same: church, then lunch at the same restaurant. It's the routines, rather than the unexpected things, that seem to remind us most of our loss. Those are the times when we may feel abandoned by our loved one. We may even feel angry with them, railing at them for having gone away and left us to cope alone. If we're honest, almost all of us will admit to having felt that kind of anger with the one who has "gone off and left us." Although it may seem terrible to be angry with someone who has died, it's a normal part of grieving. We can help ourselves immensely if we're able to talk with someone, a trusted friend, counselor, pastor, and, of course, the Lord, about our anger. Allowing ourselves to "get it out there" can help to dissipate the anger we feel so that we can move through our grief and get to the other side.

Once we've done that, we may find it helpful to make plans to change some of our routines. And, when facing a routine that can't be changed, we can determine to imagine ourselves reaching out to take the Lord's hand so that he can walk us through that activity. Those are the times when we can remind ourselves that we are not really going to church—or the movies, or to visit relatives—alone. We're going in the company of our Savior.

Friends may move away or on to other friends. People we love and who love us may eventually die. Ultimately, Christ is the only one who will never leave us, the only one we can really count on to be there for us without fail (see Hebrews 13:5).

This is a good time to begin to become particularly conscious of his presence as you move from day to day. Why not spend some time today reevaluating old routines and making plans to begin new ones? Plan to do these new routines with the Lord at your side. Then ask God to help you reach past your anger and face your pain with courage.

13 | Being Real

> *When Jesus saw her [Mary] weeping [over the death of her brother, Lazarus], and the Jews who had come along with her also weeping, he was deeply moved in spirit and troubled.* John 11:33

AY is not normally a people-watcher. Yet, when it comes to rituals surrounding death, he cannot help himself. He has observed that some of our death rituals have a surreal quality to them. It's almost as if grief draws people into a sort of drama.

Some people act the part of *the strong one*. They concern themselves with setting others at ease, with saying the right things, with creating comforting diversions. Others play *the stoic*. The stoic remains an immovable presence throughout the proceedings, like a rock, feeling nothing, saying little. When stoics are asked to voice an opinion they will generally say something like, "Well, can't do much about it. Might as well just get on with life." There are countless other roles in all their variations, but you get the point. So many people cast about for something to grab hold of in a crisis. They prefer to have their roles dictated to them by tradition or examples they have seen previously. They either don't know how to be real or they're afraid to be.

Fortunately, there is generally a much larger group of those who are content simply to be. They are aware they are likely to be sad at times. They are also aware that they have nothing to prove. They need not conjure up tears, or stuff them down in an effort to be stoic. These people are content to accept their grieving process as natural. This is an important key to healthy grieving. Give yourself permission to freely feel and express your emotions.

When Jesus found Mary and Martha weeping over the death of their brother he didn't scold them for weeping. He didn't remind them that Lazarus was now better off. He didn't spout platitudes to assuage the grief of those assembled there. He didn't try to be stoic. Instead, being deeply moved by the effect death had on humankind, Jesus wept. Can we do less?

If you've been trying to meet others' expectations by playing a prescribed role, resolve today to be real. Accept your feelings whenever they come and whatever they are and simply *be*.

14 | *Slow and Steady Wins the Race*

> *And no one ever told me about the laziness of grief. Except at my job—where the machine seems to run on much as usual—I loathe the slightest effort. Not only writing but even reading is too much. Even shaving. What does it matter now whether my cheek is rough or smooth?*
>
> C.S. Lewis
> *A Grief Observed*

*I*N this fast-paced society of ours it is tremendously tempting to think, *It's been three weeks (or months). Why am I still having such a difficult time adjusting?* The truth is, the very slowness of our healing is part of God's plan. We should shun all suggestions that we hurry and "get back to normal." The very thought is ridiculous. "Normal" has been changed forever. We can never "get back" to it. We must take the time to build, slowly and painstakingly, a new life, a new "normal."

We may also find it necessary to accept, for a season,

what some call "the apathy of grief." C.S. Lewis re-
ferred to it as the "laziness" of grief, and we might be
tempted to similarly label it. It is not laziness, however.
It is an ordinary, predictable part of the grieving process. Even animated, energetic people go through it.
Unfortunately, it is those people who are normally very
energetic and decisive who will be most tempted to
condemn themselves when they pass through this
stage.

This apathy may hit almost immediately after our
loss, or it may strike at the most unexpected, inconve-
nient time, up to months afterward. Suddenly, we find
ourselves standing in the aisle at the supermarket unable to decide between the various brands of laundry
detergent. Or we may become aware that we've been
standing in front of our closet for several minutes, paralyzed, unable to make the simplest decision about what
to wear that day. Or we may suddenly realize that we
can write our name in the dust on the coffee table and
have absolutely no desire to do anything about it. When
that happens, we will know that we have encountered
the apathy of grief. Take heart. It will not last forever. It
is simply another signpost along the road that leads to
complete healing. If we take pains to be patient with
ourselves and recognize this apathy as just a phase, it
will pass more quickly.

It has been our experience that those who fight it
prolong it. In fact, that is true of every stage in the
grieving process. When we fight the natural process,
when we try to rush through the phases of grief, when
we refuse to listen to our minds and bodies, we merely

prolong our grief. We'll make it easier for ourselves if we take the time to feel our emotions without censure, if we choose to rest our bodies rather than feeling obliged to do a forced march through each day's responsibilities, if we simply *slow down* and accept our grieving process one day at a time.

Have you been forcing yourself to ignore the signals of your mind and body in order to maintain the *status quo*? Have you been placing your sorrow on hold so that you can continue to function at your accustomed level? Have you, perhaps, even been taking on additional responsibilities in order to "stay busy"? If so, you may be avoiding rather than enhancing your process.

Spend some time today getting in touch with the very real signals your mind and body may be giving you. Those tears that spring too easily to your eyes, your desire to sleep more, your wish to simply tune out the world and sit for awhile, may be indications that you are ignoring your needs, pushing yourself too fast and too hard. Tune in to yourself today. Resolve to pay closer attention to those signals. Rather than prolonging your grieving process, as you may fear, you will actually be speeding it by meeting the needs of your mind, spirit and body.

15 The Truth Hurts —Sometimes

May your unfailing love be my comfort,
according to your promise to your servant.

Psalm 119:76

WE all hear them, those pat phrases that seem to fall so blithely from people's lips: "He's better off now." "It was God's will." "It was for the best; now he's free from suffering." "She wouldn't have wanted to be a burden."

How do you feel as you read these statements? Most people feel torn between acknowledging the kernel of truth that resides within them and the heartbreaking fact that they do not really help. Yes, it is true that if our loved one was a Christian, he or she is better off now. Yes, since we worship a sovereign God, an argument can be made to the effect that this death was God's will. Yes, our loved one is now free from suffering. And, yes, it probably is true that he or she would not have wanted to be a burden. Who would? The problem is that these phrases close the door on expressing our pain.

People most often make these statements when they feel terribly inadequate. They feel helpless in the face of death and worry that they really have nothing of substance to offer us in our pain. Or they are afraid our grief will open the door—which they have slammed shut and bolted—leading to their own grief. Generally, they're not consciously aware that they are controlling the discussion, moving it away from an area of discomfort. They may even convince themselves that they're doing it for our own good.

Unfortunately, those phrases, and all others like them, only acknowledge the more comfortable half of the truth. Our loved one has gone to a better place while we are left here to cope. She or he is free from suffering while we are left here in a world where pain and suffering are still very real, where we may feel that our friends are telling us, with these very phrases, that we—with our grief and pain—are a burden.

The truth has the ability to set us free, just as Scripture says, but only if it's the whole truth. These half-truths have a way of obstructing our healing process, of extinguishing our feelings before we've had the opportunity to express and work through them. The truth embodied in our feelings is just as valid as those other truths. It is honest to say, "I hurt more than I ever imagined possible"; "I feel abandoned and lonely"; "I miss him so much that there are times when I wish it had been me instead." These truths do not invalidate those other equally true statements. There is room enough in God's universe for both halves of the truth. Just now, we need to concentrate on the truth regarding *our* circumstances. There will be plenty of time in the future to acknowledge that our loved one is better off.

For today, quietly and tactfully tell people who remind you that your loved one is free from suffering: "That doesn't make it any easier for me right now. I still hurt terribly. But you're right. That will be a great comfort to me in the future, once this terrible sorrow has run its course." Thank them kindly and move on. You'll feel better—and heal better—for having provided some balance for the truth.

16 The Humpty Dumpty Syndrome

You feel like Humpty Dumpty. You've fallen off the wall and you know all the king's horses and all the king's men are never going to be able to put you together again. Joyce Landorf
Mourning Song

*I*N the weeks and months following the death of someone we love, we often feel like Humpty Dumpty. That's the only way to describe it. We feel broken. We hurt so much that our pain seems almost tangible. We move cautiously and uncertainly because our nerve endings are all on the alert, sensitive to the slightest stimulus. We breathe shallowly as if we're afraid to take a deep breath for fear our lungs will press too harshly upon our aching heart. There are times when the atmosphere around us seems to be charged with our own anguish and dread. We long for the days when life was simpler, sweeter.

There is a difference, however, between our King and Humpty Dumpty's. Our King is able to put even

Humpty Dumpty back together again. In fact, our King sent his Son to be broken for us so that he could put us back together better than we were before. That doesn't mean that our pain is not real. It is very real, just as Christ's pain was real when he wept for Lazarus. It does mean that we can have hope in the midst of our pain. It means that we can turn to our loving heavenly Father knowing that he will see us through this pain, knowing that Christ understands our pain because he has felt it himself.

It means that we have an Advocate and a Helper who can assist us as we grapple with the reality of death, as we struggle to find acceptance—even joy—in the face of our very personal suffering. If we are faithful to the task at hand, if we determine to walk through this storm, continually calling upon our Father-Advocate-Helper, we will arrive at the other side with a renewed understanding of our own life—and of life in general. We will learn to live more joyously because we have learned to face death.

For today, face, with courage and determination, the daunting task of examining all of the broken pieces of your life. Give full attention to the pieces of your sorrow, your anger, your fear, your disillusionment, your faltering faith. Do this, because your job in this rebuilding process is to hand each piece to your heavenly Father as he asks for them. Then watch in awe as he puts them back together in a new and better pattern of living.

17 | No Problem

Blessed are those who mourn, for they will be comforted.   **Matthew 5:4**

ALMOST every Christian who has lost a loved one seems to have at least one acquaintance who feels called upon to explain that grief and sorrow are not "of God." These people go into great detail about the tragedy *they* faced with stoicism. They tell us that they never grieved, not for one single second. God took their grief away. He waved a magic wand and it was just gone, poof!

It's always a little hard to tell whether these people are trying to encourage us or simply trying to tell us that they did it "better." Whatever their motives, the outcome is almost always the same. As these "comforters" walk away we can almost see them briskly brushing their hands one against the other saying, "There now, I told him how it's done. He shouldn't have any more trouble." These people are completely unaware that they have left the one who is already stooped under an immense load of sorrow, feeling as if they have just been waylaid somewhere along the misery road. In response to their lecture we are often left thinking, *Why isn't God doing that for me? Is my sorrow proof of my faulty faith?*

The answer, of course, is a resounding, "No, indeed!" It takes much greater faith to walk through the pain than it does to deny it. The Psalms are full of praises to God for having walked the writer through his grief and sorrow. There is no shame implicit within those psalms, only gratitude.

While Elisabeth Kubler-Ross was doing the research that eventually led her to write *On Death and Dying,* she identified the first stage of grief as *denial.* We deny that what has happened, or is about to happen, could possibly be true. We stick our heads in the sand and refuse to look at our circumstances. Yet, denial is not entirely bad. It can be a valuable tool, providing we do not get "stuck" at that stage. Denial can cushion the initial blow we suffer as the result of our loss. As denial fades in and out over the months following our loss, it can actually provide us with occasional periods of relief from the intensity of our sorrow. In those instances, denial is a gift from God. It is meant to help us through. It is only when denial moves in permanently that we must begin to worry. Then we have abused it.

Unfortunately, there are those who would have us believe that living in denial is God's preference for us. This is simply not so. If it were so, there wouldn't be so many scriptural accounts about godly men and women grieving. So, the next time people tell you that

God took their sorrow from them and they never spent one single instant grieving, pity them, for they still have their deepest grieving ahead of them. Meanwhile, be glad you're taking the *courageous* road rather than the *denial* road, and that you're getting on with your grieving process.

18 Of Laughter and Tears

I will turn their mourning into gladness;
I will give them comfort and joy instead of
sorrow. **Jeremiah 31:13**

W E get a lot of mixed messages where grief is concerned. There are those who believe that "getting on with our lives" is a sign of loyalty to our deceased loved one. There are others who believe that we are being disloyal if we don't drop everything and "honor" our dead by grieving for some set period of time. And there are people who don't want us to show our grief openly but who aren't comfortable with our having a good time either. Frequently, it can be confusing and hard to know what to do.

Those mixed messages can get all tangled up with our own needs and desires. We may feel that we need to avail ourselves of some of the help others offer, especially if we have spent a long time nursing our loved one before his or her death. We feel done in and ready for a rest, so the help is most welcome. Unfortunately, however, somewhere deep inside there may be lurking a conviction that we dare not laugh or have a good time while making use of that help for fear people will come to the conclusion that we don't really need their help after all, or that we are simply being lazy sluggards. It's as if we're convinced that laughter and grief are mutually exclusive. That is simply not true. God gave us the capacity to laugh through our tears. Sometimes those tears mixed with laughter are the most cathartic of all.

It's best, when we have such fears, to talk openly about them with our friends and family. We can quite honestly tell our friends that, just for today, we need a brief respite from our pain and the greatest help they can offer is to join with us in reminiscing about the happy times we had with our loved one. Laughter is a sign of the lasting effect our loved ones had on our lives. We've shared a great deal of ourselves with them. Certainly there were happy times.

Sometimes, in order to heal, we must free ourselves from others' expectations—and from our own. When custom has become a straitjacket it no longer serves a beneficial purpose. There will be times in the days ahead when you will actually feel like laughing. Enjoy those times. They are God's gifts as surely as is the catharsis of your tears.

19 | Why Weep?

DOES crying actually accomplish anything? Do tears serve any purpose? Or, are they simply a failing of the weak, hysterical, dependent and vulnerable?

Men, in particular, seem to have difficulty crying—at least in Western cultures. Yet there are cultures in which weeping is accepted—and expected—from people of both genders. There are many biblical examples of men weeping: David, Abraham, Elijah and Jesus were all men who were not afraid to weep in response to their grief. Weeping is a fitting response to great sorrow, regardless of one's gender.

In an achievement-driven society emotions often receive a "bum rap." Emotions do not seem to *do* anything. Our tears cannot bring our loved one back to us. They cannot help us execute our many duties following the death of our loved one. In fact, they seem to do just the opposite. It often feels as if our tears are preventing us from getting on with our life.

Recent studies have shown, however, that God's plan for our grief is beyond anything we could ever have imagined. Weeping does indeed accomplish much. Not only do our tears help to release tension, they actually carry away chemicals that build up in our bodies during times of emotional stress. In a way, our tears wash our wound.

Unfortunately, many people, especially those who were abused or neglected as children, associate emotional pain with being victimized. As a result, they feel threatened when in pain. They may even react to the loss of their loved one as if God *intended* to victimize them. Many are stubbornly determined to prove their independence and self-sufficiency because they were abused by someone they needed as children. As a result, they are uncomfortable feeling needy and vulnerable now. Their tears remind them of their wounds and vulnerability—and of their need for others and for God. Those reminders may not be entirely welcome, so we shut off our feelings and turn off our tears in an effort to protect ourselves from a threat that no longer exists.

Our fears place us in a completely untenable position. We cannot heal unless we grieve. We cannot grieve because we are frightened of feeling vulnerable. It takes great courage to surmount these fears and be true to ourselves and to our grief.

As Christians, we reap not only the physiological benefits available through our tears but a spiritual one as well. Our tears remind us of our need for our loving heavenly Father who is waiting for us to turn to him in our pain, not so that he can use or abuse us but so that he can heal and restore us. If your fear has been preventing your tears, today would be a good day to step out in courage and faith and allow yourself to weep.

20 Regrets

Peter took him [Jesus] aside and began to rebuke him. "Never, Lord!" he said. "This shall never happen to you!" **Matthew 16:22**

THOSE of us who have seen a loved one through a lengthy illness before our final good-bye often have numerous regrets. One of the most poignant regrets we may have is that we were not as honest with our loved one—or, perhaps, with ourselves—as we might have been. Like the apostle Peter, when the doctor brought the bad news we may have denied it. We may have assured our loved one, "This shall never happen to you!" But it did. We can beat ourselves up for our denial, or we can realize that we are in good company and forgive ourselves as Christ forgave Peter.

If we did not face our loved one's approaching death as courageously as we might have liked, we may have more difficulty with the denial we inevitably experience from time to time now that our loved one is gone. We may treat any slip back into a temporary state of denial as a cue to begin our mental harangue all over again. When that happens, it's important to remind ourselves that denial provides us with brief rest stops along the way, times to regain our strength and courage as we travel the road of grief.

There are times when our denial is really more of a longing for the fulfillment of scriptural promises than true denial. Our spirits hunger for the day when "he will wipe every tear from their [our] eyes. There will be no more death or mourning or crying or pain, for the old order of things has passed away" (Revelation 21:4). We may, in all sincerity, claim that promise before its time.

Many of us experience a time when we feel as if we have come to a point when God has fulfilled that promise in the present and we are comforted. We experience a sense of release from the crushing sorrow we feel. We declare that our mourning is over. We are disappointed when we find that the experience is fleeting. We may even denounce the experience as a delusion—another form of denial and self-trickery. We tend to begin mentally clubbing ourselves all over again. What we have failed to grasp is that the comfort we experienced was only meant to be a rest stop, a brief point of relief along the road.

We need to begin to trust ourselves and our grief process. And we need to trust God. If we "go with the flow"; if we trust that our experiences are unfolding as God intends, we can relax and stop bludgeoning ourselves. We can accept the brief rest stops along the road, secure in the knowledge that we are still making progress.

Determine to be more accepting of yourself and your process today. Determine to live in the moment, and embrace, with equanimity, whatever that moment brings.

21 Keeping Up

God saw all that he had made, and it was very good. **Genesis 1:31**

ONE of the most disconcerting aspects of grief is that grief never "stands still." Just when we most need it, just when we are crying out for some stability in a world blown apart, our emotional ground seems to shift perpetually beneath us. One day we may decide that the worst of the storm has passed and we can begin to get back to normal. The next day it may seem as if that good day never happened and we begin to imagine that we will never feel anything but pain.

Many of us keep trying to nail this "grieving thing" down so that we can feel like we're back in control of at least some aspect of our lives. Yet our grief just doesn't cooperate. Every time we think we finally have it in our grasp, it shifts in our hands and skitters away in a new direction. How can we keep up?

The first obstacle we need to overcome is the one presented by our own expectations. Most of us have some preconceived notion of how long the grief process is supposed to take. When we find ourselves feeling our pain and sorrow more intensely than we think we should, given the amount of time that has passed since we first suffered our loss, we are likely to condemn ourselves or assume that others are condemning us. But each of us is different. The relationship we have lost is different. Our ability to process our sorrow is different. There are a vast array of variables in our grieving. No one timetable is suited to everyone. If we refuse to mourn beyond a certain time then we are asking for trouble. Our sorrow will find an outlet regardless of our efforts to suppress it. We can be absolutely sure of that. That outlet might be a breakdown in our health. It might be angry words or actions popping up inexplicably and at inopportune times. It may be nightmares or insomnia. The list is nearly endless.

God created us to be expressive creatures. He gave us our emotions for a reason. Studies indicate that our immune system is strengthened by expressing our emotions. And recent studies indicate that it doesn't make any difference whether we are expressing joy or sadness. Both seem to have the same beneficial effect on our bodies. Does it sound like God made us that way so that he could challenge us to suppress our feelings? We think not. Our feelings are meant to act like that of a warning light on the dashboard of a car. They tell us something. When we pay attention to those lights, when we take the time to listen to our hearts and minds, we are being good stewards of the body God gave us. Naturally we need to be responsible about expressing our emotions according to the Word of God. Scriptural warnings about the expression of our feelings are there for a reason. Nowhere in the Bible, however, does it tell us to refrain from feeling. If God had wanted automatons to populate the earth he would have created them. He didn't. He created human beings with feelings. Then he saw that all he had made was very good.

Today, you can resolve to give yourself permission to feel whatever you need to, without censure. You can acknowledge that your grieving is a process of incorporating a new reality into your life. You can determine to take whatever time you need in order to complete that process. Then rest in the knowledge that God has your best interest at heart, and resolve to allow him the time to heal you according to *his* plan.

22 | *Morning by Morning*

Let the morning bring me word of your unfailing love, for I have put my trust in you. Show me the way I should go, for to you I lift up my soul. **Psalm 143:8**

ORNINGS take on new meaning after the death of someone we love. We now dread what, once, we might have greeted as the dawning of a day filled with new possibilities, new hopes, and the expected fulfillment of our dreams. Now mornings seem to slap us in the face with the cruel reality of another day spent without that one we loved so dearly. The silent house, the absence of morning greetings, the lack of cozy routines, all serve to remind us that we are missing someone important to us.

Ray remembers mornings, in particular, following his father's death. Each morning, Ray woke up hoping to hear his dad rustling the newspaper or stirring in the kitchen, making the wonderful pancakes that only he could get "just right." Ray's grief came crashing in on him fresh each morning as, once again, he perceived that nothing had changed. His memory of his dad's funeral had not been just another nightmare to be wiped away like the morning dew.

Yet God is obviously aware of our need for encouragement each morning. The Scriptures are full of people who have known grief, who have faced mornings of pain and sorrow. David spoke eloquently of his own dread of the morning when he said in Psalm 73:14, "All day long I have been plagued; I have been punished every morning." When we are hurting, mornings can indeed seem like a punishment. Along with statements like David's that tell us God is aware of our dread of the mornings, the Bible also gives many examples of healthful ways to cope with our morning misery.

In the book of Lamentations, Jeremiah demonstrates what psychologists call healthy "self-talk." While waiting upon the Lord for deliverance from his troubles Jeremiah cries out to God: "Yet this I call to mind and therefore I have hope: Because of the Lord's great love we are not consumed, for his compassions never fail. They are new every morning; great is your faithfulness" (3:21-23). Jeremiah was still in the midst of his trouble when he said those words but he chose to dwell on that which would bring him hope for a better day... maybe not tomorrow or the next day, but in God's time.

Here are some of the things David said in regard to mornings:

"Weeping may remain for a night, but rejoicing comes in the morning" (Psalm 30:5).

"But I will sing of your strength, in the morning I will sing of your love; for you are my fortress, my refuge in times of trouble" (Psalm 59:16).

Dwell on God's goodness and faithfulness today during your prayer time. Cry out to him with an expectant heart. Rest in him. And in your time of trouble, he will be your refuge.

23 Where Is God?

The existence of suffering on this earth is, I believe, a scream to all of us that something is wrong. It halts us and makes us consider other values.

Philip Yancey
Where Is God When It Hurts?

*I*N the midst of our grief many of us feel abandoned by God. In fact, that often seems to be the worst part of our grief. In our sorrow we look to God. We ask him the questions that emanate from our aching hearts: "Where are you now that I need you?" "If you are all powerful, why did you let this happen?" "If you love me, why aren't you helping me bear this pain?" At times like this, many of us feel that our questions are met with silence. It's as if, in our hour of greatest need, God takes a hike saying, "I'll come back when you're in a better frame of mind."

After his wife's death, C.S. Lewis certainly perceived God that way. In the journal he kept in the midst of his deepest grief, which was later published under the title *A Grief Observed*, he complained that God seemed to have shut and bolted the door to him. He questioned whether a god who allowed his wife's death could be a "good" god. He was forced by his grief to re-examine his understanding of God. That re-examination caused him to write: "Not that I am (I think) in much danger of ceasing to believe in God. The real danger is of coming to believe such dreadful things about him. The conclusion I dread is not, 'So there's no God after all,' but, 'So this is what God's really like. Deceive yourself no longer.'"

Are you experiencing doubts about the innate goodness of God now, while the door to him seems to be shut and bolted? In times of grief most of us do. Unfortunately, we also deny that we do, even to ourselves. It's as if we're afraid that God is so small-minded that he will not tolerate our doubts. He will become vengeful and punishing if we admit, even to ourselves, that we have questions regarding his mercy and goodness.

Is God petty and small-minded? If you're afraid to deal openly with the questions born of your grief, doesn't that indicate that, on some level, you fear that God really is petty enough to punish anyone who doubts? Our fears have a way of exposing what our hearts believe as opposed to what our heads believe. Crisis tends to bring things into focus in a way that may not happen at any other time in our lives. It is in crisis when we have the best opportunity to see clearly the chinks in the armor of our faith.

God not only tolerates our questions and our doubts,

he welcomes them. It is only when we face them that we have any hope of answering our questions and conquering our doubts. Lewis grappled with his doubts and anger toward God. He gave himself the time and the freedom to face, head on, the questions that plagued him in the midst of his sorrow. Because he did, he eventually wrote in that same journal, "I have gradually been coming to feel that the door is no longer shut and bolted. Was it my own frantic need that slammed it in my face? The time when there is nothing at all in your soul except a cry for help may be just the time when God can't give it: you are like the drowning man who can't be helped because he clutches and grabs. Perhaps your own reiterated cries deafen you to the voice you hoped to hear."

Do you have questions and doubts that you need to address in God's presence? Resolve to do so today and for as long as necessary, for when we confront our questions, our doubts, our greatest fears, we can learn to grieve not as unbelievers who have no hope, but as children of a merciful and loving God.

24 | You Just Don't Understand

Talk to me about the truth of religion and I'll listen gladly. Talk to me about the duty of religion and I'll listen submissively. But don't come talking to me about the consolations of religion or I shall suspect that you don't understand. **C.S. Lewis**
A Grief Observed

 SOMETIMES the very things people say to us in an effort to comfort us make us feel as if we've just been slapped in the face. When we're feeling as if there is no consolation, consoling words seem like a reproach. Efforts to cheer us feel like ice water down our backs. At times like that we may wish to lash out. Sometimes, we actually do, turning a blind eye to the intent behind the words. We aren't looking for comfort. We're looking for fellow travelers on the misery road. We want to know that others are there with us, not calling down to us from lofty heights, untouched by our grief, but slogging through the mud beside us. We wish to make those

messengers of comfort feel as bad as we do ourselves.

It's as if their comforting words imply that our sorrow isn't real. It feels like our comforters are patting us on the head like we're two-year-olds, telling us that we'll feel better once we've had a nap. But we're not toddlers. Our sorrow is real. We have suffered great loss and even a hundred naps won't make our grief go away.

Immediately following her daughter's funeral, in the movie *Steel Magnolias*, M'lynn, the central character, says to the friends who have come to comfort her, "I don't think I can take this. I don't think I can take this. I just want to hit somebody 'til they feel as bad as I do. I just want to hit something. I want to hit it hard!"

Does that strike a chord? It does with us. In our grief, it's easy for us to want to force the world to "be fair." We are angry, and we want everyone to experience the same kind of pain we feel. At least then, perhaps, we won't feel so isolated.

But with whom are we really angry and on whom are we trying to place the blame for our pain? God is the only being who has the power to grant life. God is the only one who could have prevented the death of our loved one. Is it all right to be angry with God? We think it is. Are you afraid that God will retaliate if you are honest with him regarding your anger? God understands. He knows our thoughts better than we do. We may as well confess them to him and deal with them openly. God prefers honesty to artificial spirituality and platitudes. If he is our "Abba-Father," our "Daddy-

God," then we can share with him our deepest secrets, our anguished cries, without fear of reprisal.

Christ came to earth to experience all that we have experienced so that we would have an advocate in heaven who has felt our pain and our sorrow. Christ understands from experience the realities of living in a world contaminated by sin and death. God understands our grief. He will not abandon us in our pain. He can handle even the most acid emotions spilled out in his direction.

Don't hold back. Tell God what you feel. He will lovingly accept you just as you are, anger and all.

25 Anger—The Second Layer of Emotion

> *I loathe my very life; therefore I will give free rein to my complaint and speak out in the bitterness of my soul.* **Job 10:1**

THERE are no better biblical examples of sheer, unadulterated anger than those of Job. He hurled accusations at God, calling him names and spitting out his rage. Are you tempted to follow suit? Are you so angry with God that you cannot imagine why you ever believed in God's goodness and mercy? If so, you are in good company. Many mourners feel that way, at least for a while.

Anger is always an emotion that is layered atop some other, deeper emotion. Our anger may emanate from feelings of guilt about something we did or didn't do during our loved one's life. If our loved one helped to provide us with some of our identity in the world or financial support, we may be feeling insecure. We may be feeling betrayed because God allowed our loved one to die. We may be feeling frightened of being alone, and frightened of death itself. We are most assuredly feeling lonely and abandoned. Any of those feelings may be at the root of our anger.

We can work through our anger by identifying the underlying emotion and talking it over with God. We may also need to dispel our anger through some physical means like walking, hitting a punching bag or pillow, cycling, working in the garden or pruning trees. Any physical exercise is likely to help.

We can also seek out an understanding friend or family member with whom we can talk about our anger, being careful in our selection of such a person. Not everyone is comfortable listening to someone vent his or her anger. If we can find no one close to us, a counselor might be a good choice to listen to our expressions of anger.

As we deal with our anger, however, our most effective ally, by far, is God. Does that surprise you? So many of us are taught that anger is an unacceptable emotion. We assume that God is least likely to listen to us when we are angry. It's important to remember that God gave us the capacity to feel anger. God did not turn his back on Job when Job expressed his anger. God will not turn his back on us.

So, tell God how you feel. And listen carefully for his reply. It is only when we speak freely with our loving, heavenly Father about our anger, and all of our other emotions, that we can be fully healed.

26 | *The Eternal "Why?"*

No man has power over the wind to contain it; so no one has power over the day of his death. **Ecclesiastes 8:8**

DEATH has a way of causing us to face our absolute powerlessness. Humans would prefer to pretend that we are powerful. After all, we can send rockets to the moon. We can irrigate the desert. But the truth is, we have no more power over death than we do the wind. We are helpless in the face of death, and many of us rail against that helplessness. We want to *do* something. We want to *make* the pain stop. We want to make God answer the question *"Why?"* Did I do something wrong? Am I being punished? Has God stopped loving me? Did God ever love me? If he loves me, then why?! Why me? Why now?

All of these questions tend to march relentlessly through our minds when we are grieving. When we lose a loved one many of us go through a crisis of faith in which we question everything we have believed until now. Unhappily, a lot of people who are questioning feel as if their questions indicate that they are bad Christians. This is simply not so. C.S. Lewis is widely hailed as one of the most profound theologians of this century. He was a man who knew what he believed and why he believed it. Yet his wife's death cast him into crisis. Lewis' search for answers to the questions spawned by his great loss is profiled in his book *A Grief Observed*.

Regardless of how others may have handled their personal crisis, however, we are each called upon to come to peace with our own feelings of helplessness. No one can do that for us. And in the final analysis, no one can show us *how* to do it. It is a battle for peace that can only be fought on our knees. We may rail at God. We may tell him how unfair we think he is. We may tell him how terribly angry we are with him. In the end, though, we must find some way to face, as did Solomon, the fact that only God can tame the wind and only God has a wisdom so perfect that he can rightly determine when a person should go on living and when that person must die. It is only when we surrender our anger, our grief and our heartfelt "Why?" that we can know that peace.

On some level, we may fear that accepting the death of a loved one may seem like being glad for it. But that's not true. Part of our acceptance, however, will probably include the fact that God is using our loss to purify our faith and we can be glad for that. He is using it to teach us lessons we might not otherwise learn. He is not teaching us to be happy about our loss but he is redeeming it. God can transform the worst tragedy imaginable if we allow him.

During your prayer time today, honestly tell God how you feel about your loss. Tell him *everything* you feel. Ask him your questions. Tell him about your anger. Weep before him. Then ask God to give you peace—in his time.

27 | Can We Grieve and Still Believe?

> God washes the eyes by tears until they can behold the invisible land where tears shall come no more.   **Henry Ward Beecher**

*U*NFORTUNATELY, there are those who believe that faith and grief don't mix. They tell us that if our faith in God is strong and mature we will not "waste" our time on grief. But there are many places in the Scriptures where biblical figures grieve the dead. David grieved the death of his son, Absalom. Joseph grieved the death of his father, Jacob. The nation, Israel, grieved the deaths of Aaron and Moses. In fact, sackcloth and ashes seemed to be the order of the day in those instances. Were those people being faithless?

Naturally, our sorrow is uncomfortable. Most of us would rather not have to endure it. Some of us are so anxious to avoid it that we seek scriptural grounds for doing so. We decide that since we can't control death we can at least control our feelings about it. We try to prop up our feeble efforts to short-circuit our pain by saying that we are being "people of faith." But people of faith accept God's will for their lives. They allow themselves to experience the feelings that God has given them, because it was God who created us with the ability to feel our emotions—even our pain.

It is true that emotions without faith can ravage us. Sorrow without faith is hopeless. Anger without faith will destroy us. We need to be able to take it to God. Grief without faith isolates us. But grief *mixed* with faith engenders a relationship with our heavenly Father. When we are in pain, but we have the hope that God is with us in our pain, that eventually our pain will be relieved, that we will grow and move closer to God as we learn to take our distress to him, we can bear it more easily. We are still grieving, but it is grief in the context of our relationship with God, and that makes it possible to endure everything.

Most important, though, our faith makes it possible for us to lay claim to the promises of the Scriptures. Those believers whom we have lost in death are merely asleep (1 Thessalonians 4:13-18). Because we know that we will see our loved ones again one day, we can say with conviction, "Where, O death, is your victory? Where, O death, is your sting?" (1 Corinthians 15:55).

Faith makes it possible for you to rest in the confidence that God will meet you at the point of your distress and walk with you through the storm.

28 | The Death of Our Dreams

> *I pray also that the eyes of your heart may be enlightened in order that you may know the hope to which he [God] has called you.* **Ephesians 1:18**

IN the course of living with a person it is inevitable that we should expect to share our future with him or her. God has given us the ability to imagine the future. It is a strength that allows us to anticipate an assortment of future possibilities thereby increasing our chances of adapting successfully. Unfortunately, when someone we love comes to an untimely end, that strength can work against us. When a loved one dies, we not only lose that person and his or her immediate input in our lives, we also lose our dream of a future together.

Our lost hopes and dreams seem to be a greater source of pain when we have lost a child. When Lynn lost her first baby within hours of her birth she was most devastated by the loss of her hopes and dreams for that child's future. She had not had the opportunity to get used to the baby's presence in her life. She did not miss her in the traditional sense. Yet, Lynn knew that she would never bathe her baby. She would never feel her snuggle against her neck. She would never hear her first laugh or her first word. She knew that she would never tuck away that first lock of hair or press her first corsage. There were so many things that she would never experience with that particular child. Lynn sensed even then that no matter how many other children she might have in the future, there would always be an ache in her heart that would only be healed when she finally held her daughter in heaven.

When we lose someone we love, whether it is a child, a mate, a parent or someone else close to us, we need to grieve not only the loss of that loved one but also our hopes and dreams for the future. Once we grieve what might have been we will probably still find ourselves stopping from time to time to think about the way this event or that holiday would have been different—if only. If we have grieved adequately, however, we will experience only a short time of regret before we are able to move on. We can use those moments of regret to remind us to lean on God's Word. We live in the present and we must make the most of what God has given us for today. We have the hope that God will wipe away every tear because his Word says so (Revelation 21:4). We know that Christ came to give us eternal life so that the power of death would have no hold over us (Revelation 1:18). These are verses, along with many others you may find, that you can cling to in hope. Then wait expectantly for the day when the trumpet will sound and you will meet your loved one in the air along with Christ himself (1 Thessalonians 4:17).

29 | *On Wearing Masks*

No greater burden can be borne by an individual than to know that no one cares or understands.   Arthur H. Stainback

*F*OR a time after Ray's dad died many family friends inquired how Ray was doing. He always replied, "Just fine. Things are going okay." But what he was really thinking was, *I feel awful and it feels like no one really cares. Why are you asking me? My dad just died. How do you think I'm feeling? Isn't it obvious that I'm miserable?*

Because Ray was only twelve when his father died, he didn't trust himself to discern between those people who were inquiring about his well-being out of courtesy and those who truly wished to give him emotional support, so he gave the same answer to everyone. But it isn't just twelve-year-olds who don't feel able to discern the difference. When we are deep in our grief a gray gloom seems to hang over everything, clouding our perceptions. Often, we don't quite trust our judgment. We hesitate to "wear our hearts on our sleeves" for fear

of embarrassing ourselves or the one making the inquiry. So we get into the habit of choking down our pain, even when we're with those who genuinely care.

Often we are motivated by a desire not to be a burden. Our grief is so overwhelming that we fear it will overwhelm those around us. We choose to spare others from our sorrow. That may sound noble but there is a basic flaw in that kind of thinking. We forget that they are perfectly capable of taking care of themselves. We don't have to do it for them. We deprive them of the privilege of comforting and ministering to us when we constantly wear a mask, censoring our responses to their inquiries.

Others of us may choose to smile and make the best of it because it's just too scary to admit how vulnerable we're feeling. We may mistakenly believe that our pain will go away if we ignore it long enough. Or, we may be attempting to protect ourselves from others' inept efforts to be comforting. Even the best intentions cannot spare us from the hurt we may feel when someone makes an awkward attempt to be sympathetic. Sometimes it seems easier to grin and bear it alone than leave ourselves open to that sort of hurt. In the long run, however, the isolation we feel will be far more painful than the momentary hurt caused by a thoughtless remark.

Naturally, there are times when it is wise to wear a mask. It would intensify our pain if we laid ourselves bare at the most casual inquiry regarding our well-being. With practice, however, we can learn to discern between a casual question and a heartfelt desire to be helpful.

Most of us have a few trusted friends with whom we can honestly share our deepest feelings. It is up to us to develop the habit of honesty when we are with those chosen few. It may be hard to put away the mask we wear in public but it is essential to our emotional health. If we are faithfully honest with our trusted friends, soon we will be healed enough that we will be able to dispense with our mask altogether.

Until that time we need to remember that we must never wear a mask in prayer. God knows our hearts. He knows our minds. He desires complete honesty from his children. Whether we are angry or questioning his goodness or whether we are lost in a sea of hopelessness, God is near. He waits with open arms for us to fly to him and weep within the warmth of his embrace.

Spend time today telling God everything that's on your heart. Allow your loving heavenly Father to comfort you as no one else ever can.

30 Forgiving Ourselves

> *It is a great grace of God to practice self-examination; but too much is as bad as too little. Believe me, by God's help we shall advance more by contemplating the Divinity than by keeping our eyes fixed on ourselves.*
>
> Teresa of Avila

*I*T is nearly inevitable that we will go through intense self-examination following the death of someone we love. But our self-examination can too easily turn to self-flagellation. We are all human and our relationships have unavoidable ups and downs, thoughtless words and painful times. We all have regrets.

For one who is mourning, however, self-recrimination seems almost unavoidable. We ask ourselves a hundred questions. *Was there something I could have or should have said to make things better between us? Why didn't I say "I love you" more often? If I had done things differently, could I have prevented his death? Should I have made a fuss every time he lit up a cigarette? Should*

I have insisted on driving her to her meeting instead of listening to her when she insisted that she felt well enough to go alone? What if I had called the paramedics sooner? Would he still be alive? What if I had insisted that she see the doctor despite her objections? Would I still have her here beside me? It is when these questions haunt us that we are most aware of the finality of death. We are aware that there are no second chances. We can't try it again and get it "right" this time. We can't take back those hurtful words and set the record straight. We are simply left with our aching need to find some way to forgive ourselves.

Yet, even as we struggle to forgive ourselves we may be hearing condemning retorts within our own minds. Did she really mean so little to me that I can just forgive myself for what I did or didn't do? Can I really be that cavalier? Do I really deserve to be forgiven? If I forgive myself am I being disloyal to him? Am I being callous to the hurt I caused?

It's so easy to condemn our part in the difficulty while canonizing our loved one. We would rather take the full blame upon ourselves than take an honest look at the relationship as a whole. Lynn's friend, Anna, blamed herself for a while after her husband's death because, even as he was having a heart attack, he insisted that it was nothing, it would pass, and told her repeatedly not to call for paramedics. With hindsight, of course, she could see that she should have ignored him. It was much easier for her to blame herself for not having been omniscient than it was for her to blame him for being pigheaded. Most of us have been well-schooled with regard to "speaking ill of

the dead." It seemed unthinkable even\ to refer to her beloved husband as pigheaded, despite the fact that, where his health was concerned, the term *pigheaded* was an apt description. Yet, Anna couldn't bring herself to be "disloyal" to him, just then, by describing him so.

Weeks later, when she received the autopsy report and realized that he had had a series of heart attacks over several years, each of which he had ignored, she finally allowed herself to feel the anger she had been dodging. She learned to call him pigheaded without guilt. And, gradually, as the sting of her great loss faded, she began to say the word pigheaded with love in her voice. It was one of the qualities that had endeared him to her. He had seen his family through numerous hard times because he had refused to quit when other men would have.

Because Anna was finally able to face *all* of her memories of her husband, she kept his memory alive in a healthy way. She was able to tell her grandchildren about their beloved grandpa—both the good times and the not-so-good ones—so that they could grow up with the image of a man who was to be admired but not worshipped. What a wonderful legacy.

In order to keep your loved one's memory truthful and real, you must forgive yourself and accept the forgiveness that God makes available to all of us through the death of his Son, Jesus Christ. Then, forgive your loved one as well.

"Godly sorrow brings repentance that leads to salvation and leaves no regrets, but worldly sorrow brings death" (2 Corinthians 7:10).

31 | *Sweet Relief*

You can't heal a wound by saying it's not there! Jeremiah 6:14, (TLB)

GRIEF brings with it such a mixture of feelings. We may feel anger and rage over being abandoned. We feel pain and sadness over our loss. For those of us who have nursed our loved one for a period of time preceding his or her death, we will very likely feel relief—sweet relief. We are relieved that the one we love is finally out of pain or misery. We are relieved to have finished the arduous daily task of ministering to the needs of someone who may not always have been in the best of moods, certainly someone whose physical and emotional needs, in addition to other of life's duties, stretched us to the limit.

Unfortunately, most of us do not really feel free to admit that we are relieved. We feel so disloyal, so whiny, so ashamed. Somehow we associate feelings of relief with happiness. If we admit our relief it's as if we're saying we're happy our loved one is dead. Yet, if we're perfectly honest, some happiness enters in. We are not leaping for joy over the death of our loved one, of course. But we can be happy that he or she is finally out of misery and has finally gone to meet the Lord.

If you spent time nursing a loved one with a terminal illness you may have spent long hours praying for physical healing. Yet death for a Christian is the ultimate healing. There is none better. You may also have prayed for some respite from the difficult days you faced while nursing a sick or elderly person. It is perfectly all right to be relieved that those days are finally over. You may have done every chore set before you with gladness, but that does not mean you cannot be comforted by the fact that now you are finally finished.

In order for us to be able to process our relief and the secret shame we may feel over it, we must face it squarely. We must be honest with ourselves and at least one or two others who we feel will understand. If we refuse to acknowledge our relief we force the feelings that may accompany that relief into hiding. When those feelings of relief and shame are hidden we cannot deal with them, and that creates a potential for an "infection" to develop within our wound. We cannot scrub what remains outside our perception.

That does not mean that we need to force ourselves to hurt by tearing our wound open every chance we get in the misguided belief that we are speeding our healing by doing so. It does mean confronting our feelings honestly—all of them. It means accepting our feelings as neither good nor bad. Feelings fall outside the realm of value judgments. It is only the things we do as a result of our feelings that can be judged.

So resolve, today, to accept your feelings without judgment while carefully assessing the actions you wish to take in response to those feelings. Determine to allow yourself the luxury to feel everything that's in your heart, not just the emotions you deem praiseworthy. Rest in the Lord and in the goodness of his creation, joyful in the knowledge that his creation includes the emotions he gave you.

32 | A Fragrant Offering to the Lord

If I must suffer pain
Before, in death, my life is gained.
Let my life be poured
A fragrant offering to the Lord.

If I must suffer loss
Then purge my life of all its dross.
Allow my life to be
A fragrant sacrifice to thee.

Lynn Brookside

THERE are times during our grieving process when we are absolutely sure that we will never again feel anything but sorrow. Lynn certainly felt that way immediately after the loss of her child. Afraid to openly express her sorrow with tears and even more afraid to express her anger, she stuffed them down inside where they festered, creating an enormous emotional infection. That infection poisoned every relationship, every moment of her life, until the time when she was able, finally, to accept what had happened; until the time when she was able to say to the Lord, "Let my life be a fragrant sacrifice."

God is faithful. He takes our suffering—when we allow him—and uses it to make our lives a fragrant offering. King David went on to make all the preparations for the building of the temple after losing more than one of his children. The apostle Paul continued to encourage and exhort believers after he was imprisoned. After her husband's death, Ruth, a Moabite woman, helped her mother-in-law, Naomi, return to Israel, and Ruth became a part of Christ's lineage as a result. The list goes on and on.

There were many times during Lynn's grieving process when her Christian friends tried to tell her about God's faithfulness, just as we are telling you now. Until it was possible for her to truly listen, her response was always the same: "I don't want to be a sweet smelling sacrifice if it means losing my daughter. I would pay any other price, but not that. I didn't sign up for this kind of pain. This is too much. I can't live with this hole in my heart."

If that's how you're feeling just now, we understand. So does God. He is not only faithful, he is patient. He will continue to call to you, through your pain, and despite your pain. There will come a day, sometime in the future, when you will suddenly realize that you are ready to answer that call; when you will find that you are ready to say, "Lord, make my life a fragrant offering." When that happens, be grateful for God's patient, consistent call, and grab hold. He will take you the rest of the way.

33 The Curse of Silence

> There is no monster like silence. It grows faster than children, filling first a heart, then a house, then history.
>
> **Roger Rosenblatt**
> **"The Freedom of the Damned"**

ONE of the greatest regrets Lynn has regarding her family life is the silence that followed any great loss, whether it was the loss of her baby or a loss of much less magnitude. So many of us are taught not to talk about our wounds. We absorb the message, spoken or tacit, that "talking doesn't help," "weeping doesn't change things," "talking about it will just make you sad." None of those statements is true. Talking does change things. Weeping does help. Talking about our sorrow does not increase our sorrow; it purges our sorrow.

Silence is a curse to injured, hurting people. Silence tapes up our wounds before they have been thoroughly cleaned so that they are sure to become infected. Talking provides at least a portion of the cleansing we need for our wounds.

Unfortunately, the belief that it's better not to talk about things that may cause us to feel sad is a pervasive one. Too many people try to keep the conversation light whenever they are with someone who is grieving. They steer the conversation away from our lost loved one and try never to mention our loved one's name. We may begin to wonder if we are the only ones who remember that he or she ever lived at all.

Our friends and acquaintances may also be attempting to spare themselves our sadness by avoiding painful subjects because they are not comfortable with the intensity of our emotions. Our good friends, however, will try to overcome their discomfort when we explain that we need to talk about our loss. It may not seem entirely fair that we must be the ones to take the initiative in this but it is true that, usually, we must.

When we do, we may find it necessary to assure our friends that we will not come unglued if we weep; we will not suffer permanent damage if we sob; we will live through this pain—if we are allowed to talk about it. We should also feel free to assure them that, although we are taking our fears, worries and sorrow to the Lord regularly, their listening ear is still necessary to our healing. God created us to need both kinds of fellowship. We can remind our friends and family members—not accusingly, but forthrightly—that relationships die from neglect far more often than people do, and silence is a form of neglect, sometimes the most awful form of neglect imaginable.

If you have been walled in by silence, today is a good

day to pull down those walls. Find someone to talk to. If your friends and family members are unable to accommodate you, or if you are far from home, find someone else with whom to talk. Make an appointment with your pastor or a counselor. Seek out a support group for the bereaved. Find a way to break your silence—and heal.

34 | Is God Trustworthy?

> *Though you have made me see troubles,
> many and bitter, you will restore my life
> again; from the depths of the earth you
> will again bring me up. You will increase
> my honor and comfort me once again. I
> will praise you with the harp for your
> faithfulness, O my God; I will sing praise
> to you with the lyre, O Holy One of Israel.*
>
> **Psalm 71:20-22**

F OR many years after Lynn lost her baby she found herself unable to trust God. Oh, she was willing enough to obey him. That did not change. But she did not feel able to truly trust him. She became extremely cautious in her prayers. She tried not to ask too much of God. She viewed him as a mercurial being, at best, so she schooled herself not to expect to have her prayers answered. She hoped that, in time, God would miraculously heal her pain and answer her agonized "Why?" so that she could easily trust him again. But that did not happen. She was frustrated when she finally realized that she would have to learn to trust God *despite* her pain and doubts. Yet, that is exactly what God asks of each of us.

Learning to trust God in spite of our pain and doubts is a lifelong task. It takes discipline and humility. It takes a constant acknowledgment that we, in our human frailty, do not know what is best for us. It takes a continuous reaffirmation of the fact that God, and God alone, is sovereign. He owes us no explanation for the circumstances of our lives.

Lynn discovered that it was her pride that kept her asking, "Why?" It was her pride that kept her demanding explanations from God. When she thought to herself, *I would have done it differently. I would have been loving enough to let me keep my baby*, she betrayed her pridefulness. Eventually, she was forced to acknowledge that she was not qualified to judge God's love.

Lynn also felt despair. She often felt as if she had no reason to go on living. Sometimes, she wondered whether God cared about her at all. Other times, she questioned God's very existence. In time, Lynn learned that despair is a spiritual problem. She needed to confess it to God and ask him to take it from her. She found it necessary to combat despair by declaring God's Word to be true and by confirming God's goodness and mercy, regardless of her feelings at the moment.

Do you find yourself hedging in your prayer life, trying not to ask too much of a God you no longer feel you trust or understand? Has your loss caused you to wonder about God's goodness and mercy? If so, perhaps you will choose to make a statement of faith like the one made by the Psalmist who, though he had seen "troubles, many and bitter," knew "you will restore my life again;... I will praise you... O my God."

35 Our Labor Is Not in Vain

The sting of death is sin, and the power of sin is the law. But thanks be to God! He gives us the victory through our Lord Jesus Christ. Therefore, my dear brothers, stand firm. Let nothing move you. Always give yourselves fully to the work of the Lord, because you know that your labor in the Lord is not in vain. 1 Corinthians 15:56-58

WHEN we are still in the midst of our grief we may be tempted to think that it is unfair to be subjected to the sting of death when we are no longer under the law. Because we know that we have been released from the law and given victory over the powers of darkness through our Lord Jesus Christ, we may want to ask why God has allowed death's sting to touch us. There is no easy answer to that question. It seems flippant to respond to such a heartfelt question, born of grief, with the simple statement: "We live in a fallen world which has not yet been fully redeemed." But that really is the only answer.

As Christians we must deal with the disparity between our lives in the present and the hope of what is to come. We possess the promise of a bright future yet we live, move, and work in a world that groans while waiting in eager expectation for the sons of God to be revealed and all of creation to be set right (Romans 8:19, 22). We ourselves groan inwardly also as we wait for that glorious time (Romans 8:23). God must be particularly touched by that groaning when it comes from one who is grieving the death of a loved one.

At moments like these, we reflect upon the marvelous promise about the full manifestation of our adoption as children of God and the redemption of our bodies (Romans 8:23). We also need to remember that this redemption is a process. In that process, we need to focus on the task God has given us to do. For now, that task is grief work.

Does that surprise you? So often we think of "God's work" as the missions or teaching Sunday School or some other worthwhile but narrowly focused project. In actuality, the fundamental task God has given us to do is the working out of our salvation (Philippians 2:12). That may include missions work or teaching Sunday School or any of a number of other projects we may undertake in the Lord. Yet surely part of the work that we must do, as we strive to grow in Christ, is to deal honestly with our grief. That is the labor which God has set before us for a season. And we have God's assurance that we do not labor in vain.

36 Committed to Healing

Forget the former things;
do not dwell on the past. Isaiah 43:18

As hard as we try to overcome the chaotic effects of our loss, we are inevitably tempted to seek shelter in the solace of the past. It seems to be a place of refuge and safety, a far more predictable place than the one we now occupy.

But there is an inherent danger in seeking the comfort of the past. The more we ruminate upon the past the more we alter it. Not deliberately, certainly. But alter it we do. We have the power within our minds to make our past over into whatever we choose. The more we choose to dwell in the past, the more we tend to imbue it with the power to provide us with the things we desire. If we continue along that path, eventually the past becomes a mirror of the present. The more pain and unhappiness we feel in the present, the more joyous and pain-free the past seems to be. Many of us are sorely tempted to "medicate" our pain with our memories by retreating into them whenever the pain gets to be too much. But this "medication" impedes our healing because, in this instance, a certain amount of painful "scrubbing" is necessary to the healing of our wound. The longer we postpone feeling that pain, the greater the risk that an emotional infection will set in. That infection will poison us and make our eventual healing all the more difficult.

If we are truly committed to our healing, we must face the past—all of it. And we must strive to face it realistically. Most of all, however, we must endeavor to move from the past and dwell in the present, even with all of its pain and heartbreak. We need to establish an atmosphere of prayer in our lives that will allow us to be open to God's presence and to make room for the thoughts he would have us think. It has been said before, but let us say it again. There is no way to the other side of this storm but through it.

This day commit yourself to feel your pain for the moment, process it for as long as necessary and, eventually, move on.

37 | Feeling Abandoned

> *Our earliest separations... have given us all our first, bitter foretaste of death. And our later encounters with death—with death down the road or with death knocking at our door—revive the terrors of those first separations.* **Judith Viorst**
>
> *Necessary Losses*

ALL of us have experienced separations that we felt might kill us. Most of us don't remember the first time it happened but it is almost guaranteed that, sometime during our very early childhood, our mother—or other beloved caretaker—was forced to leave us for a period of time. We might have been left in the church nursery or at home with Dad while Mom ran to the store or with Grandma while Mom went to "go get" our baby brother or sister. It is likely that we were well cared for in her absence, but the most wonderful care in the world could not make up for the fact that our mother—our security—was missing.

Each of us is left with some residual fear of abandonment as a result of these experiences regardless of how beautifully our mothers may have cared for us the rest of the time. For some that residual fear is minimal. Some have slightly greater fears as the result of events that may very well have been completely beyond our mothers' control. For others of us who had frightful experiences of abandonment, our fears may be nearly paralyzing. Losing a loved one can cause all those old fears to resurface, sometimes forcefully.

For those who have great fears of abandonment, losing a loved one can cause our life to become rife with anxiety and dread. There is no greater abandonment than the "forever" kind. We may actually feel engulfed by our fears, completely without hope. It can be extremely helpful if we realize that this feeling of being overwhelmed may have its roots in early childhood.

Children feel things with their entire selves. When they are hungry, they are hungry in every cell of their being. They "become" hunger. When they are sad, they are completely without hope. They know nothing but sadness. If early feelings of abandonment are triggered by a loss in the present, our reaction may seem—even to us—to be out of proportion because those feelings have their roots in the early years of our life, when all of our feelings were magnified by our youth and lack of life experience.

Knowing that there is an explanation for what's happening to you, however, may not be enough to get you through. If you find yourself unable to talk and pray your way through your fears; if everyday challenges and experiences seem to strike fear into your soul, nearly paralyzing you no matter how hard you try to tell yourself they should not; if you seem to be in a state of high anxiety every minute of the day, it would be wise to seek counsel from someone you trust, someone who is trained to help you cope with these early issues. It is possible to heal. God will walk with you, even through this great fear. The time you spend dealing with these early issues will yield a reward far greater than you can ever imagine.

38 | The "Good Old Days"

What's too painful to remember,
we simply choose to forget.

From *The Way We Were*

(Columbia Pictures, Rastar Production)

R AY knew a woman named Rebecca who lost her husband a few years ago. Rebecca's husband was killed in a car accident that resulted from his own drunken driving. Rebecca had been through many trials with her husband as a result of his drinking problem. She sat through his funeral, in ever-increasing shock and anger, listening to people eulogize him. She said there were times during the service when she wanted to get up and take another look in the casket to make sure they were talking about the right man. It was maddening for her to hear such pretense.

Unfortunately, Rebecca had been taught as a child that it's unacceptable to speak ill of the dead. As a result she had no way to vent her anger and frustration regarding the manner in which her husband had died or the hurt he had caused her during his life. She felt that she must simply "forget" all of her hurt and anger, never speaking of it to anyone. Naturally, her bottled-up feelings made her miserable.

Finally, in desperation, Rebecca sought counsel, where she experienced a great deal of anxiety, even then, over speaking negatively about her husband. Ray had to keep reminding Rebecca that she was simply speaking the truth.

After some time, Rebecca was able to lay the past to rest. Once she had vented her negative feelings toward her husband she was gradually able to remember the good times in their marriage, before his drinking had changed their relationship. Eventually she was able to acknowledge that "sometimes he was a jerk, but I can forgive him for that. There were good times too." Her new realism enabled her to process her grief more healthfully than she had previously.

Although most of us do not have such weighty issues left dangling when we bury our loved ones, a great many of us lay our loved ones to rest with some kind of unresolved issues still nagging at us. Inevitably that nagging will grow more persistent if we feel constrained to remain silent about those issues rather than work toward their resolution.

We need to acknowledge the all too prevalent idea that we must not "speak ill of the dead" as the superstition it is. Hundreds of years ago people really believed that their loved one's ghost was hanging around listening to all they said. They believed that the ghost would claim retribution if they said anything derogatory about the deceased. As Christians we know better, yet many of us are still uncomfortable "speaking ill of the dead," if for no other reason than that we do not wish to appear unloving. If we use the Word of God as our standard, however, then we know that we are called to speak the unvarnished truth, in love. To do less not only dilutes a biblical principle, it obstructs our grieving process.

Even if we are not afraid to speak negatively about our loved one, we may be tempted to idealize the past because we are trying so hard to come to peace with it. Or it may be an honest effort to see God's hand in our character development, his persistent, faithful way of providing for us in the midst of crisis. We may simply be trying very hard to remain positive about some extremely negative events.

If that's the case for you, it's important to give yourself permission to acknowledge all of the truth. Today, determine to trust God to use even the bad memories to refine and teach you. Then tell someone you trust about some of the negative feelings you may still have toward your loved one. You will grieve more healthfully as a result.

39 | *Feeling Like a Leper*

An odd by-product of my loss is that I'm aware of being an embarrassment to everyone I meet.... Perhaps the bereaved ought to be isolated in special settlements like lepers. **C.S. Lewis**
A Grief Observed

CRISIS has a way of separating our friends and acquaintances into two camps: those who are committed to seeing us through and those who cannot cope with our crisis. It can be a rude awakening when we find that some of the people we thought were our closest friends suddenly make themselves scarce when trouble hits. It can be equally surprising when we find that some of the people we never really considered close come to our aid and comfort.

As if we are not already enduring enough uncertainty, now we have to endure the changes in relationships that inevitably take place following the death of a loved one. Lynn's friend, Kirsten, says she sometimes has a mental image of herself sitting next to a heap of doll-sized people, sorting through them, separating the ones she can count on to be there for her from those who have disappeared from her life.

It's not as if our friends planned it this way. It's not even as if they consciously choose not to be supportive. Whatever the reason, something within them simply does not allow them to be there when we most need them. In times like these, many of us find that we are called upon to grieve the loss of friends in addition to the loss of our loved one. It is hard not to be bitter about it. It doesn't seem fair. But bitterness will only hinder our grieving process. It is better, when we can, to talk openly about our hurt and disappointment with our friends.

It can also help if we try to keep in mind that our friends probably still love us. They may never have had a grief of their own and feel completely unequal to the task of seeing us through ours. Or, our grief may remind them too much of their own unhealed wound. Perhaps their inability to see us through this crisis may have its roots in events that took place in their lives so long ago that they do not even remember them. Whatever the reason, we are left with the task of picking up the scattered pieces of our lives and moving on in the company of those who are committed to being there for us in our need. We can take solace in the fact that the Lord will never leave us nor forsake us. And we can thank God for those friends he has given us who are willing to see us through.

We will need to release those other friends from our expectations. Releasing them may be difficult but it's necessary to our continued healing. We also need to commit ourselves to processing all of our pain, that which derives itself directly from the death of our loved one and that which may have its roots in the abandonment we feel we are enduring from some of our friends. If we are courageous enough to acknowledge all of our grief, perhaps, when our friends need us in the future as a result of their own crises, we will have healed so completely that we will be one who will see them through... with God's grace.

40 *Dreams in the Night*

The fragments of my broken heart
Lie sealed within my chest
Shattered like fragile crystal
Cast carelessly upon a stone.

I go slowly...

Looking not unlike my fellows, yet...
Lungs burn within me,
Breathing shallowly for fear they
Push too harshly upon the shards.

Quiet! Please, quiet.
Do not speak too loudly.
You may disturb the sleeping
Memories of my love.

And doing so...

My love will walk again
Within my dreams and...
Waking can only cast my heart
Once more, upon that stone.

Lynn Brookside

$\mathcal{M}$ANY of us have dreams about our loved ones for a period of time after our loss. Most often in these dreams our loved ones are still alive, still—or again—vibrant. These dreams are usually nothing more than a reflection of our intense desire to repudiate our loss. Our grief may have become so much a part of our waking moments that we strive for a respite from it during sleep.

Naturally, our minds do not turn off when we are asleep, but there is a difference in the way we process information while we sleep. All of our inhibitions are suspended and our internal rules are modified during sleep. We will entertain thoughts in our dreams we would never entertain in our waking moments. As a result, it is not a cause for concern if we dream of brawling with our deceased loved one. It is probably nothing more than a reflection of our anger at having been left behind, abandoned.

Sometimes we may have dreams of our loved one returning to instruct us as to methods for handling a present-day problem. This is likely just a reflection of our unconscious mind's ability to process and propose possible solutions to problems that are worrying us. Our unconscious mind takes on the identity of our loved one in order to arrest our attention or, sometimes, simply because we miss him or her so terribly.

Sometimes, however, we will dream of our loved one doing something completely out of character. Lori Anne dreamed of her deceased husband weeping uncontrollably. She was dealing with a great deal of residual anger with her husband because he had been so emotionally unavailable during his life. She was intrigued by her dream because she had never actually seen her husband weep. Upon reflection, she concluded that he had been more wounded than she had ever consciously realized. God used that insight to bring about further healing for Lori Anne. Suddenly she had an explanation for her husband's emotional distance, and while that did not heal all of her wounds, it did make it much easier for her to forgive him and lay her anger aside.

Whatever the content of our dreams, it is important not to assign too much significance to them. Chances are, they are nothing more than a manifestation of our intense desire to have our loved one restored to us. In time and with healing we will cease to have such dreams. In the meantime, we can treat our dreams as God-given opportunities to further process our sorrow.

41 | *Wanting them Back*

It's funny how we love to talk about Jesus raising Lazarus, but what we never seem to consider is that at a later date Lazarus died. He did not live forever. We don't know how many years his miraculous stay of death lasted, but we know for certain he did die.... I particularly wonder what Martha and Mary's thoughts were when he died a second time. Joyce Landorf
Mourning Song

WHEN a loved one is not taken suddenly but, rather, by a lengthy illness or disease, some Christians heap recriminations upon themselves. They wonder why their faith was not enough to heal him or her. They miss that person so much that all they really want is to have their loved one back and they are not particularly focused on the future cost of that desire. It may help you to process your sorrow better if you take a realistic look at that cost.

If we were truly able to bring our faith to bear in

order to restore our loved one to his or her former life what would the cost be? Our loved one has already been through the process of preparation for death. Would we want him or her to have to go through that preparation again? Death comes to everyone eventually. Would we want to lose our loved one to death once more?

Because none of us has the power to restore our loved ones to their former lives these questions may seem ridiculous, and rightly so. When we stop to think about them, they are ridiculous. That's why it's important for us to examine even the fleeting thoughts, the ones that flit through our minds, torturing us on the run. When we take them out and really look at them, often, we can chuckle at them, robbing them of their power to torment.

What thoughts are you shoving away so quickly that you are not consciously aware of their sting? Maybe it is not a wish for a return of your loved one. Maybe it is something as innocent as wishing you had bought him or her that favorite game or trinket he or she always wanted. Perhaps it's wishing you had gone on that vacation you always planned but never got around to taking. Whatever those fleeting thoughts may be, are they really worth torturing yourself? In the grand design of the universe how important is that trinket? How would that vacation spot compare to heaven? Do we really believe our loved one is concerned with a vacation now that he or she has gone to be with the Lord?

Those of us left behind have a way of torturing ourselves with earthly concerns while our loved ones are prepared to bask in a Light that outshines the sun. Today would be a good day to become aware of your thoughts, especially the ones that rush through your mind at such speed that you feel their sting without any conscious awareness of their message. Examine the ones that are tormenting you with their implicit "if onlys." Hold them up against the truth of God's Word... and laugh.

42 I Feel Your Pain

For we do not have a high priest who is unable to sympathize with our weaknesses.... Let us then approach the throne of grace with confidence, so that we may receive mercy and find grace to help us in our time of need. **Hebrews 4:15-16**

SOME of us are so afraid of the intensity of our emotions when we first lose someone that we hide our pain away for years. It comes as quite a shock when, later, we stumble across those same intense feelings. Somehow we have assumed that those feelings will dissipate if we ignore them long enough. It's a surprise when we find them just as we left them, waiting to be expressed in their full force.

It was certainly a surprise to Lynn when she discovered her reservoir of sorrow. As a child she had been convinced that the open expression of emotions was indicative of an inferior human being. Having grown up in a home where any display of emotion was frowned upon she did not feel free to express her grief over the loss of her baby. Before she could open the floodgate to her pain she needed to comprehend the inherent error in that sort of thinking. Her pain and sorrow lay waiting for her to arrive at such a place, not without consequence, obviously, but they did wait.

By the time Lynn was ready to face her grief she had developed a really wonderful support system. Her close friends and associates were an immense help during the period of time she spent, finally grieving. Despite Lynn's growing acceptance of her emotions, however, she sometimes wavered in her conviction that expressing them did not indicate that she was defective. Whenever she faltered she found it helpful to talk openly about her doubts and fears.

On one occasion she found herself tearfully expressing some of her anguish to her friend and mentor Alan Brown. Despite the fact that he was always totally accepting of her and her feelings, she couldn't help wondering if he must not think just a little less of her for feeling such deep anguish over something that had happened so long ago. Yet the depth of her pain forced her to go on, expressing her distress, bleeding off some of the extreme pressure of emotions too long neglected. As they stood to leave their meeting place Lynn felt compelled to inquire as to Alan's frame of mind. As they hugged good-bye she asked in a quiet voice, "How do you feel about someone who would act this way?" She expected—hoped for—some judgment from him. She wanted him to tell her that she was not defective. She would even have accepted a mild rebuke, a statement to the effect that she needed to rein herself in and not get so worked up over things. Alan wisely refrained from making judgments. He simply answered, just as quietly, "I feel your pain."

That simple statement is one of the greatest gifts one person can give another. It is more profound than all the soliloquies, all the poems, ever written about death and sorrow. It does more than any other four words anyone can say to a grieving person. No other words are as comforting. No other single sentence does more to break down walls of isolation formed by deep sorrow and regret. When those words are merged with a touch or an embrace, they mend the heart and lift up downcast eyes. They tell us that we are not alone in our grief.

Is it any wonder that God sent to us a human Savior? He knew we needed to be absolutely certain that one member of the Godhead fully comprehends our pain and, if one member knows, all three know, for they are One.

When we're feeling as if our grief will be the end of us and we're tempted to rail against God and all of creation because our pain just *will not stop*, if we listen, we can almost hear our Savior saying, "I feel your pain."

And so do countless others. You are not alone. We feel your pain too. Today, determine to turn a deaf ear to the inner voice that may be attempting to convince you that people who openly express their feelings are inferior. Instead of listening to those messages, choose to have the courage to share your grief with someone who loves you and who will embrace you and say, "I feel your pain."

43 | Letting Go

My eyes have grown dim with grief; my whole frame is but a shadow. Job 17:7

MOST of us have known or heard about people who seem to place their households in suspended animation after the death of someone close. They leave their loved one's room untouched, bed made up and ready for their return. The loved one's books and papers are set out on the desk as if they had just stepped away momentarily. It is almost as if those mourners are waiting for God to come to his senses and return their loved one to them.

These grief-stricken people who simply cannot let go seem to feel as if accepting their loss is like abandoning their loved one. It seems to them that acceptance implies approval, even gladness, regarding their loved one's death. They don't realize that they will continue to be victimized by their loss until they've come to accept it.

You may not be living in the past, spending your time existing in your memories, but most of us experience a reluctance to let go. We need to assess, realistically, the consequences of our reluctance. The past is static. It does not adapt to our present needs. Our memory of those pleasant times when our loved one brought us joy will not nurture us or meet our needs in the present. Furthermore, we will become increasingly isolated if we continue to exist in the past while those around us are moving on with their lives.

When we refuse to let go of the past we are, in essence, saying to God, "Your timing is wrong and I don't accept it. I have a better plan and I'm not going to let you get away with this. It hurts too much and I don't trust you to walk me through this pain."

Job had a similar complaint. Job questioned God's judgment, accusing God of committing an injustice by allowing Job to be afflicted when he had done nothing wrong. God responded to Job's complaints saying, "Where were you when I laid the earth's foundation?… Who marked off its dimensions?… Have you ever given orders to the morning, or shown the dawn its place?" Job was forced to reply, "Surely I spoke of things I did not understand, things too wonderful for me to know" (see Job 38-42).

It's the same for us. When we rage against our loss we are questioning God's judgment. We speak of things we do not understand. Naturally we are angry because death overtakes us like a storm, usually without warning. We are helpless to stop it. But we will continue to feel victimized by it until we let go. Letting go doesn't mean forgetting our loved one or being glad for his or her death. It does mean accepting God's will for our lives and bowing to his sovereignty.

If you feel that you are ready to say a final good-bye to your loved one, today would be a good day to plan a farewell ritual. Write your loved one a letter. Express how much you miss him or her. Describe your sorrow over the death of your dreams for the shared future you will never have. Then sign the letter and say good-bye.

If you are not yet at a point in your grieving process when you can let go, mark this page and come back to it when you are ready.

44 Putting Our World in Order

Not until each loom is silent
And the shuttles cease to fly,
Will God unroll the pattern
And explain the reason why
The dark threads are as needful
In the Weaver's skillful hand
As the threads of gold and silver
For the pattern which He planned.

Author Unknown

THERE are people who eliminate every visible vestige of their loved one just as soon as the funeral is over. Unlike those who keep all their reminders set out, untouched, as if they are awaiting their loved one's return, these people believe they can shorten their grieving process by making their loved one "vanish." Both extremes are unhealthy. People who dispose of every reminder, every memento, every article of clothing, are bound to regret their actions later. It would be far better to store those things away for a time, if possible. Eventually, we are going to want to be reminded of that person who was such a big part of our lives. If we have disposed of everything, it will be too late.

When we lose someone we love, we have sustained the greatest emotional wound possible. Psychological tests designed to determine the number of stress points in a person's life assign different numerical values to various types of stress. A birth in the family is worth so many points, a job change is assigned a different number. A minor illness or injury is given yet another number. The death of someone close to us is assigned a full one hundred points. That means that someone who has *absolutely* no other stresses in his or her life is automatically catapulted to the top of the scale by the death of someone that person loves. Needless to say, when we look at it that way, it seems fairly apparent that it is not a good idea to make any major decisions for a while after our loss.

Of course there are times when it cannot be helped. If a person dies without a will and there is no mortgage insurance, the one left behind is likely to have to make some serious decisions regarding whether or not to attempt to hold on to the family home. When a parent of young children dies, the parent left behind must make some essential decisions regarding childcare and the like. These decisions simply cannot be avoided. When we have a choice, however, it's a good idea to postpone any major decisions during the first year following our loss. All the decisions we make during that first year will be colored by intense emotions. In addition to the fact that we are not in a frame of mind that makes rational decision-making likely, we will be adding still more stress to our already stressed-out minds and bodies. So be kind to yourself, do not try to make major changes in your life just yet.

If a decision simply cannot wait, ask God to clear your mind and give you wisdom. And find someone you trust who can help you with it, preferably someone who will pray with you about it as well as discuss it with you. Obviously, you will not want that person to make the decision for you, but you will do well to get some responsible feedback before you make the decision yourself. In the meantime, put off any decision that you can reasonably postpone. Focus, instead, on your healing. There will be time enough for the rest once you have begun to regain your equilibrium.

45 | Medicating the Wound

As a mother comforts her child, so will I comfort you. Isaiah 66:13

ONE of the decisions that grief-stricken people sometimes find most difficult to postpone is the decision to form a new relationship. In the months following the loss of the love of our lives we are particularly vulnerable. The loneliness we feel is beyond anything we could have imagined. We hurt so profoundly that we may find it difficult to function. We long for the time when our loved one soothed us and made us feel safe. Sometimes we feel adrift on a sea of sorrow. At times like these, we tend to make decisions based on our intense desire to minimize our pain, feeling an immense need to be comforted and nurtured. We may even be seeking to replace the object of our love. It's important, however, to avoid new romantic relationships during the early stages of our grief. Much as we might wish it, a new relationship will not "medicate" our wound. It will only serve to confuse and delay our grieving process.

Often it's a good idea to set a time before which you will refuse even to consider a new relationship, although that time limit will differ from person to person. Some may be able to consider a new relationship as soon as six months after their loss, although that is certainly the earliest date at which it might be wise to do so. Others will want to wait two or three years. It depends entirely on the person involved.

Whatever you choose to do, it is paramount that you give yourself time to heal. If you do, you'll find that time well spent. And, when you're ready to pursue a new relationship, you'll find it will be stronger because you waited. Your new relationship will be free from the weight of issues left over from your former relationship. You will be truly free to seek a new life without unresolved grief causing you to stumble over things that would not otherwise have been a problem. You will be free to have a new life because you have taken the time to fully release your old life.

You need not remain alone and uncomforted, however, until the time when you are ready to begin a new relationship. Take this time to become increasingly close to the Lord by remaining in prayer and in his Word. Take solace in the promise of comfort from the Lord and from his people.

 *It Wasn't You*

I thought I saw you today
Standing there in the checkout line
Just out of reach.
I started to call your name
But I stopped.
My mind said it wasn't you,
Couldn't be you.
My heart said otherwise,
Vehemently.

I was embarrassed by the
Tears that sprang, unbidden
To wash away my
Disappointment.
I wrestled—like Jacob with the angel—
Until I had conquered, once more,
My grief.
The struggle left me feeling
Out of joint.

The world slipped away
As I left the store.
There was only me
And my grief.

No you.
Never again a "you."
Finally, I grabbed my grief
By the neck, shouting,
"I will not let you go until you bless me!"

Lynn Brookside

SOMETIME during the weeks or months following our loss, most of us experience a fleeting instant when we believe we have seen our loved one. It may be in a check-out line or on the street or in the half-light of a movie theater. Wherever we are when it occurs, it cannot help but reawaken our great sorrow. Tears spring to our eyes and we are once again completely and painfully aware that we miss our loved one more than words can ever express. We would give anything to have him or her back. We wrestle with our grief. We want our pain to stop. We want our sorrow to be over.

It's tempting at times like these to feel angry with ourselves. We say that our mind is "playing tricks" on us. We imagine that it has aligned itself against us and we wonder if we are deliberately making ourselves miserable. Why else would we make such a devastating mistake?

It's likely that this case of mistaken identity is just one more way we have of reminding ourselves of the reality of our pain. It is far too easy to belittle our pain. We may even have convinced ourselves that our pain is insignificant, our grieving process unnecessary. Then it happens. The back of someone's head, the way he or she walks, sends us scurrying. We rush ahead to catch a glimpse of the person's face, hoping and praying it will be our loved one and we will be able to declare that we have only had a nightmare. Yet we know all the while how fruitless our effort will be.

It happens so quickly that it's impossible to retell the incident without sounding completely insane. Of course we knew all along it wasn't really our loved one. Of course we know how silly it all sounds. But, for just a second, our heart leaped in hope. We were invigorated by the promise of release. It's in the moments following such an incident that we need to remind ourselves that this time of grief serves a purpose. God created us with an inherent ability to heal, and our grief process is designed to bless us with healing. It is in those moments when we need to take our grief by the neck and shout, "I will not let you go until you bless me!"

47 Taking a Break

Death and the sun are not to be looked at steadily. **La Rochefoucauld**

ONCE we have committed ourselves to our healing process some of us make the mistake of becoming too single-minded about it. We become overwhelmed and our efforts are counterproductive if we are not careful to strike a balance. We dare not spend all of our time processing our feelings. In order to heal we must leave time to work, time to reflect, and time to play. We will work more successfully if we take the time to renew and refresh ourselves before we face the next challenge.

Grief does not present us with a uniform, step-by-step path. We will not move smoothly from one stage to the next. Our path will be full of experiences typified by the one step forward, two steps back theorem. Sometimes we can prevent ourselves from backsliding too far by taking a well-deserved break from the stresses of our lives. Our emotional health depends as much on knowing when to take a break as it does on knowing when to grieve. We are not suggesting that you distract yourself during the difficult moments in order to shut out the pain. That would be unhealthy and, ultimately, destructive. We are suggesting that you pace yourself by planning to take breaks from your grief.

Even Jesus took time to get away and renew himself in prayer. Jesus knew that if he didn't get away from the hustle and bustle of life, sheer fatigue might cause him to lose his sensitivity and perspective on life. The same is true for us. We need to keep our sensitivity and perspective if we're going to obtain the greatest healing.

Although prayer is one of the best ways to refresh ourselves, it is only one of many. We may want to take a walk and enjoy the healing touch available throughout God's creation. We may want to do something with our hands, paint or sculpt or sew. We may want to write something completely separate from our grief journaling, a children's story or a limerick. There are countless possibilities. The point is to find something to do that's relaxing and refreshing, something different.

Today would be a good day to begin a list of leisure time activities you'd like to do. Then, the next time you feel the need for a break, consult your list... and enjoy!

48 Saying Good-bye

I did not know how hard it would be to say good-bye. Yet it was harder still, when I refused to say it.

From the diary of a grieving widow

THERE comes a time when we all need to say good-bye to the one we have lost if we are ever going to close the door on our past and walk confidently into the future. If we do not have the opportunity to truly say good-bye, we are deprived of what counselors call "closure," which means exactly what it says. In this case, it is a completion or conclusion to our former life with our loved one. Until we have closure we will never be able to move on in our lives. There will always be a part of us that's "back there," in the past.

For those of us who wait years to say our good-byes, it's a particularly painful process. There may be many reasons for our delay. At the age of twelve, Ray did not have the resources or the knowledge to fully grieve his father. He had to wait years before he could achieve closure on his grief. Sometimes people are unable to make it to their loved one's funeral, which leaves them with an unfinished feeling. In the past, when a woman's baby died people mistakenly believed that a mother's grief would be lessened if she never had the opportunity to see or hold her child, that she would be better off if the body was simply "spirited away." This caused most bereaved mothers to feel that their grieving process could never really be complete. And sometimes, we are simply not ready to say good-bye until many weeks or months after our loved one has died.

The act of saying good-bye seems to make our loss "real" somehow, and until we say good-bye we find all kinds of ways to hold out for a better ending to the story. We hold our emotions in suspended animation awaiting our loved one's return. We hold on to a thread of hope that we will wake up one morning and he or she will be there, waiting for us. It's terribly painful. Yet, many believe that saying good-bye will be even more painful. And in a way, it is. The difference is that while our good-bye is dreadfully painful, it allows us to move past our pain and into healing. Our refusal to say good-bye merely prolongs our pain and prevents our healing.

Our lack of closure will eventually result in attempts to shut out our pain. Most people don't realize, however, that attempts to block out the pain also often block out memories of our loved one. Our memories fade, even the happy ones, because we are striving so hard to make the whole awful truth vanish.

If you have not yet said good-bye, today would be a

fine day to do so. Write a letter to your loved one. Tell him or her everything, not just the good things. Tell your loved one that you are angry, that you are lonely, that you wish he or she had remained alive long enough to witness this event or that. Pour your regrets into that letter. If it's possible, take it to the cemetery and read the letter at your loved one's grave. If not, plan some other ritual of closure. Read the letter aloud and then burn it or bury it or make a ceremony of sealing it in an envelope and storing it away. Pray that God will enable you to fully accept his will for your life, including this loss. Once you've done that, turn your face toward the future, with expectation.

49 | Facing Death

> *Our denial of death makes it easier to walk through our days and our nights unmindful of the abyss beneath our feet. But denial of death will also... impoverish our lives. Because we replace death fears with other anxieties. Because death is so interwoven with life that we close off parts of life when we shun thoughts of death.*
>
> **Judith Viorst**
> *Necessary Losses*

A LOT of people become obsessed with thoughts of death once they have lost someone close to them. For a period of time following our loss every good-bye may seem to bring with it thoughts like "Will this be the last time I'll see this person? He could be hit by a car on his way home today." Or we think, "Is this the last time I'll walk on the beach? I could die of a heart attack tonight in my sleep." It seems as if almost all of our thoughts revolve around death and dying. If we voice our thoughts, friends and family often accuse us of being morbid, but that's not usually the case. We are simply manifesting a heightened awareness of one of the aspects of being human. Death is as much a part of life as birth. We spend a lot of time denying that fact but it still remains. Nothing can change it.

In part, this preoccupation with death, reported by so many, is nothing more than a reaction to our previous denial of death. It is simply the swing of the pendulum. Knowing that, we can trust that the pendulum will continue to swing, seeking a middle ground when the time comes. Ultimately, that swing may set us more right than we were before the death of our loved one.

Our heightened awareness of death can help us to appreciate life. It teaches us to treasure our relationships, to voice our love for others more often than we may have previously. It can help to reawaken our senses. We learn to tune into them, to value the richness of our experiences. We are aware of how precious every moment is. As Emily, the central character in Thornton Wilder's stage play *Our Town*, says when she is granted the chance to re-experience one day of her life after she has died, "It goes so fast! We don't have time to look at one another. I didn't realize. So all that was going on and we never noticed."

Of course we, as Christians, have a different view of death from the one presented by Wilder. But there is a certain emotional truth represented in his work. Most humans do not "realize life while they live it—every, every minute." When someone we love dies, if we are

very attentive, very willing to learn from our experience, we are in a position to realize life. We are suddenly acutely aware of the preciousness of "every, every
minute." We are also in a position to become conscious
of our need to serve the Lord faithfully and with gladness "every, every minute," because the time we have
on this earth is limited. If we allow our thoughts about
death to turn us to an appreciation of the preciousness
of life and the urgent need the world has for the message of salvation, rather than allowing it to turn us
toward fear, our lives will be enriched beyond measure.

50 | *Anniversaries*

It's over now.
The house resounds with the terrible noise
Of water pipes, footsteps and flies on
*   window panes.*
In the upstairs nursery are the most
*   dreadful sounds.*
Silent, aching sounds rise up from cold,
*   white sheets.*
While her pillow cries out,
Crushed beneath her absent head.
Over by the window, an irregular flutter.
As a potted Easter flower,
Faded ribbon 'round its neck,
Looks out at summer children racing by
And weeps its petals, one by one,
*   to the floor.*   **Lynn Brookside**

SOME of our greatest challenges in the years following the loss of a loved one are the anniversary dates. Wedding anniversaries, birthdays and holidays all have the potential to open our wound afresh. For Lynn, it is Easter. Each time she sees an Easter lily she is reminded of the beautiful baby daughter she lost. Even the less significant dates can thrust us back into the midst of our pain and feelings of loss. It may be the opening of football season or fishing season or some other date that no one else would even be aware of. Each person's needs will be different at these times. There is no one best way to handle these anniversary dates. We need to commit ourselves to healing according to our own pattern, our own needs. We need to allow our grieving, always an individual process, to follow its course. When we do, we will heal, not by our own efforts but according to God's plan.

It is the anniversaries more than anything that help us to come to grips with exactly what we are missing now that we no longer have our loved one with us. It is the empty chair at the table on Thanksgiving, the missing pair of helping hands during Christmas baking, the missing watermelon carver on the Fourth of July that bring to mind, once again, the depth of our loss. Each special date gives us another opportunity to process some of our pain. When you think about it, it's just as well that God's plan for us includes dealing with our loss a little at a time. Otherwise, we would be overwhelmed.

We will need to anticipate our heightened need for the company of others as well as for time alone with the Lord as these anniversaries approach. This is not wallowing in our pain. It is simply taking care of ourselves in a realistic way. We may wish to ask those who are close to us to keep us company; not so that we can distract ourselves with people and busyness but so that we will not have to be alone. We can even invite people to join us in a happy time of reminiscence if we are comfortable with that idea. However you choose to observe anniversaries and holidays, give yourself permission to look back and remember, always mindful of the fact that we live our lives in the present. Allowing yourself to grieve at these special times isn't a sign that you are losing ground. It is simply an honest acknowledgment of your great loss.

If you have a special date approaching, make plans now to be extra kind to yourself. If you don't, mark this page and come back to it as your next anniversary date draws near.

It's the Little Things

> There are "firsts" you can brace for 'cause
> you know they're coming. But there are
> more firsts than the anticipated ones. One
> "first" that caught me off guard was the
> first time I saw my dad's handwriting
> after he died. I routinely opened my bank
> statement and found a deposit slip he had
> filled out for me. Such unexpected, unpre-
> pared for, firsts can be real two-by-fours
> between the eyes.   **Sandy, a grieving daughter**

GRIEF presents us with an array of
paradoxes. Following the death
of our loved one we look out over the landscape of our
lives and mentally make special preparations to deal
with the major landmarks that lie before us. We anticipate the difficulties involved in scaling the mountains.
We foresee the pain we will experience in traversing the
valleys. It's the little things that seem to hit us blind-
side, causing us to dissolve into a heap, figuratively, if
not in reality. We may find that selling the old family

home is not nearly so difficult as sitting at the dinner table in the presence of an empty chair, or going to the mall without our faithful shopping companion. Death has a way of underlining the importance of the little things in life.

It's hard not to feel guilty when our emotional responses seem so topsy-turvy. We feel embarrassed and try to make excuses for ourselves. It may help to know that we are not alone. Our experience is a common one. It will also help if we can stop calling these events little. They are not. The entire fabric of our life has been rent. It will never be the same. If we deal forthrightly with our sorrow over each of these "little" moments we will find that we are able to grieve better, more fully. Our grief process is not a unit we can take all in one lump. It's multi-faceted, made up of small moments of grief joined together to create a whole—a sparkling jewel of healing.

We need to resolve to work through the feelings as they come, regardless of how insignificant the event may be that triggers our sorrow. We can journal, talk, weep and pray through these moments, anything that will get us through to the other side. The only requirement placed upon us by our desire to heal is that we claim our right to feel our emotions.

It's also important to realize that these little things do not take God by surprise. All the events of our lives were well known to him before our lives even began (see Psalm 139:16). Trust God, who can and will use each event, both the little ones and the big ones, for our ultimate good.

52 Shared Sorrow

I can't cry, because every time I cry Dad cries and then I feel like I'm rubbing salt in his wound. I tell myself that it's his wife that died. I should be more understanding. But, she was my mother! I wish to heaven I could find some place to grieve!

Lani, a grieving daughter

I T is a rare thing to be the only one grieved by the death of a loved one. We usually find ourselves one of many. We must find a way to grieve in the company of others who hurt differently but just as profoundly. That fact can be both a comfort and an annoyance. It's wonderful, at times, to be able to discuss our pain and share our reminiscences with those who are feeling similarly. It's also frustrating, at times, especially when another member of our family seems to be overwhelmed by his or her own pain so that we feel we dare not share our burden with them for fear of overloading them.

An even greater problem develops when we are

attempting to deal with our grief head-on while other members of our family are striving to remain encapsulated in denial. We become angry because they seem to be blocking our attempts to heal, and they become angry because it feels to them as if we are rubbing their noses in the sorrow they keep trying to avoid. Sometimes, sparks fly. There is no easy answer for this sort of dilemma.

When this sort of stand-off develops we must weigh our choices carefully. If possible, we need to discuss, openly, our feelings regarding the manner in which our family members seem to be dealing with their loss. We can pray with them. We can state our need to face our pain honestly. We can suggest that they do the same. In the end, however, our family members must deal with their own grief in their own way and in their own time. We must simply see to our own grieving process without carrying our family's excess baggage in addition to our own.

If we find that we are spending too much time dealing with our family's interference in our grieving process we may have to tell them, in no uncertain terms, to cease and desist. That, however, should be regarded as a last resort. If, after discussing the problem openly, our family members continue to undermine our attempts to express our emotions honestly, it may be possible simply to agree to disagree. They may not be able, at this point in time, to face their pain as squarely as we have chosen to. If we can ignore their attempts to interfere with our need to express our pain then that seems the best choice. If we find it impossible to ignore their interference, we can ask God to bring us a friend or friends with whom we can be open and honest about our feelings in a place set apart from our family. This is much more difficult if we are actually living with our family, but it is not impossible.

Whatever we do, it's essential that we continue to process our grief, regardless of our family's attempts to ignore the issue. Once we have successfully navigated through our storm of grief we will be better equipped to help our family members navigate through their own storms when they finally choose to. We cannot recover for anyone but ourselves and we must continue to process our grief regardless of the cost. The cost of remaining in denial is bound to be much higher.

53 *When Young Children Grieve*

"Let the little children come to me, and do not hinder them, for the kingdom of God belongs to such as these...." And he took the children in his arms, put his hands on them and blessed them. Mark 10:14, 16

---

*W*HEN there are children in a family that has lost a loved one they will need a special kind of care. We need to approach their wounds with particular gentleness and empathy. Children especially need to be encouraged to grieve openly and for as long as necessary. We don't want to give them the impression that they must grieve in a certain way or for a particular length of time, for children will grieve as individuals just as adults do. But we do want to help them grieve to whatever extent and in whatever way they are able.

A child's response to death will be affected by age, personality type and his or her perception of death. In many instances, very young children regress to more infantile behavior after the death of a loved one. They may not understand the permanence of death but they will still need help in verbalizing the sorrow they feel due to the loved one's absence. When we sense that young children are struggling with feelings for which they have no labels we need to be sensitive to the cues they give us. If a child who does not generally throw temper tantrums begins to do so after the death of a loved one, we may say to him or her, "I guess you're feeling very angry right now. I miss Daddy (or whomever) too, and that causes me to feel angry sometimes also. What makes you the most angry?"

If, after such a loss, a child is easily moved to tears, we can talk about our own sadness and how natural it is to feel that way. While it's essential that we allow children to cry or cling to us or do whatever they need to, for as long as they need to, we also need to assure our children that, although it may not feel like it just now, their feelings will fade away. They will not always feel this way.

If you discover in your conversations with your child that he or she is bargaining with God for the return of the loved one—as children often do—you will want to talk about our need to trust God's judgment even when we do not like or understand what has happened. Like adults, children will not be able to accept their loss and move on if they are still bargaining.

It's helpful to ask questions that will elicit conversation. Give your child numerous chances to talk about his or her feelings. Wait patiently for your child to reply. Children need more time to think through the entire subject of feelings because they lack life experience with them. A child who is able may admit that he or she is angry with Mommy for leaving, or with God for "taking her away." A younger child may be only vaguely aware of the fact that *something* is wrong. It's helpful to such children if we provide labels for their feelings regardless of whether we think they are old enough to fully understand. We must also be prepared for children to re-experience the trauma of their loss when they are older and better able to process and verbalize their feelings. One little girl who lost her grandmother when she was four suddenly dissolved into hysterical weeping one day when she was six. She had finally reached a stage of development when she was able to grasp and verbalize the magnitude of her loss.

If you have young children you will need to commit yourself to assisting them in their grief. The way their feelings are handled at this tremendously important juncture will affect them for the rest of their lives. Remember to remain constantly in prayer, and trust God to use your efforts to help your children "pick up the pieces." God has a heart for children. Healing is his plan for all of us but particularly for the children.

54 *When Older Children Grieve*

All your sons will be taught by the Lord, and great will be your children's peace.

Isaiah 54:13

OLDER children and teens will probably grieve in much the same way adults do, but teenagers especially will feel their grief much more profoundly. Adolescence is a time when all emotional reactions are heightened. We must not assume our teenagers are simply being overdramatic. We need to be there to listen to them. We need to give them permission to feel and responsibly express their emotions—all of them—not just the ones that feel more comfortable to us.

When a widow does not weep "for the sake of the children," her children may interpret her lack of tears in a negative way. They may doubt her love for their father and, by extension, her love for them. That may sound ridiculous, but it happens—often. It's essential to remember that if we treat our own emotions matter-of-factly, our children will not be frightened when we express them. In fact, they will probably be comforted to know that they are not alone in their feelings. We need to assure our children, however, that they are not responsible for taking care of us when we are feeling sad or angry. We can assure them that this, like all feelings, will pass, and it will not hurt us or destroy us to feel this way for a time. We can assure them that their feelings will not hurt or destroy them either, although teenagers, in particular, often feel as if they will.

When adolescents experience an immense loss, like the death of someone very close to them, it is particularly important to be aware of their tendency toward depression. Listen for cues that may indicate that your teen is feeling isolated or suicidal. If that seems to be the case, talk to him or her immediately. Do not simply hope that things will work out given time. Remind your teen that suicide is a permanent end to a temporary problem. It is tremendously easy for teens to convince themselves that they would not be missed if they died. Assure him or her that you would be desolate if he or she were gone. Speak plainly and forthrightly. Tell your teenagers lovingly, yet in clear, declarative sentences, that you do not want them to hurt themselves. Pray with them. Assure them of your support. Teens often do not want to add to a parent's load in time of trouble so they may hold back and refuse to talk. Help them list—at least mentally—people they can talk to about their feelings if they do not wish to talk with you. Ask your teens' permission to talk with their youth pastor and tell him or her about the loss your teen has recently suffered and explain the need for additional support. Consult a counselor who has experience in working with teenagers if you have any reason at all to believe a counselor might be necessary.

Regardless of a person's age, the angry feelings of protest, the hurt, the longing for the way things were, the sadness, the guilt, the worries, and the fears all need to be talked out. Children and young people simply need to be given more than the usual permission and encouragement to do so. Their grief is substantial whether or not they are capable of verbalizing it effectively.

If you have children it will be necessary for you to carry a double load for a time. In the midst of your own grief it's essential that you also give time and attention to the grief your children are experiencing. With love and an abundance of prayer, you will grow and mature together as a result of your time of grief. Remain committed to one another and seek God's face at every opportunity.

55 Looking for Someone to Blame

> The web of our life is of a mingled yarn,
> good and ill together;
> our virtues would be proud
>   if our faults whipped them not;
> and our crimes would despair
>   if they were not cherished by our virtues.
>
> **Shakespeare**
> *All's Well That Ends Well*

W HEN we lose a loved one, many of us search for someone to blame. Were the doctors at fault? Did the paramedics miss an important clue? Would my child still be alive if the police had arrived more quickly? Was my husband distracted by something when the accident occurred? Did my wife ignore her symptoms because her mother told her not to worry about them? We may be harassed by such questions. We want—demand—an explanation for what has happened to us. One woman plagued the county coroner until she finally wrenched a statement from him to the effect that, perhaps, the doctors had not quite outlined her mother's treatment as well as they might have. Somehow, she believed that if she could just find the cause for her loss, she could be at peace. Generally, in cases like that, we achieve little peace even when we do find someone to blame. We cannot change the unchangeable. We have lost our loved one and there is absolutely nothing that will bring him or her back.

It can be helpful to step back and analyze what it is that's actually fueling our desire to fix blame. If we're honest, we'll admit, in most cases, that anger is the answer. In some unusual cases, those in which incompetence or negligence is genuinely involved in our loved one's death, our anger can be turned to some good. For example, anger is sometimes the catalyst for necessary change in hospital policy, governmental regulations or with those who set and administer policy and regulations. Usually, however, our anger is simply a manifestation of our grief. Anger is a normal stage through which virtually all of us must pass as we travel the path of our grief.

If you have been looking for someone to blame you may want to stop to consider your motivation. Talk it over with someone if you feel confused about whether your anger is warranted or simply a phase of grief. Take your anger to God and talk it over with him. If, in the process of praying about it, you discover that some of your anger is really with God, talk that over with him too. He will always listen.

If you have been searching for the party responsible for the death of your loved one, today would be a good day to assess where your anger is coming from. If there is a genuine need for you to take action in order to set things right you can decide what those actions should be. Once you've done that, you will be free to travel down your path of grief unfettered. Your trip will be easier because you have made the effort to come to peace with the truth about your loss—whatever that truth may be.

56 | *Putting Guilt in Its Place*

Therefore confess your sins to each other and pray for each other so that you may be healed. James 5:16

GUILT seems to be an almost unavoidable part of the grief process. Just as there are those who try to find someone else to blame for their loved one's death, there are those who would never dream of laying blame anywhere but on themselves. Sometimes, although fairly rarely, the survivor's guilt may be justified. When that appears to be the case, that person is in need of compassionate teaching with regard to repentance and forgiveness. In the vast majority of cases, however, guilt is completely unfounded. When Ray's father died, he, like all children, wondered whether he was not being punished for having been "bad." Perhaps his father would still be alive if he had been a "better" boy. Ray had only the most nebulous idea how he might have been better and no idea what he might have done that was bad enough to deserve to lose his father. He was, nonetheless, overcome by guilt.

Others have similar stories to tell. It's not only children who wonder whether they are being punished when they lose someone they love. Almost all of us, child or adult, are conscious enough of our inherent sinfulness that it is not difficult for Satan to fulfill his role as the accuser. Taking full advantage of our vulnerability following the death of our loved one, Satan preys on our pain, whispering his accusations in our ear, transmuting our ragged emotions into guilt or condemnation.

In either case, whether or not the guilt is justified, we can be assured that we need carry it no longer. God calls us to confront our guilt. He wants us to face it and deal with it decisively according to the plan outlined in his Word. He does not instruct us to do this in order to keep our emotional wound open and bleeding. Rather, he does it so that the wound can heal cleanly, without risk of infection. James 5:16 gives God's simple instructions for abolishing guilt.

If you are bowed under a load of guilt over things you did or did not do while your loved one was alive or if you are blaming yourself for your loved one's death, or some element that contributed to his or her death, follow God's simple instructions for dealing with guilt and talk it over with someone you trust. Then, take it to the Lord together. Ask God to relieve you of your guilt, whether it is real or imagined. Leave your burden at the foot of the cross and turn to face this new phase of your life free from guilt and condemnation, secure in the righteousness imputed to you through the shed blood of our Savior.

57 Surround Yourself with Life!

> When my dad died, people sent flowers to us. After a week or so, the petals started falling off and the leaves were shriveling. I remember my mother saying, "Now I have to deal with something else dying."
>
> **Sandy, a grieving daughter**

WHEN our sorrow is new, everything seems to remind us of our loss. We see that loss reflected in a hundred different ordinary elements of our lives. That's why this is a good time to make an effort to bring living things into your home and work space. Buy some potted plants or go to the animal shelter and get that pet you've always wanted. An aquarium is not only full of life but is restful also. If you do not have the time or energy to care for actual living things right now, then buy a few posters or paintings that are representations of things that are full of life. Best of all, surround yourself with friends and family who love and care for you, not all the time, but often enough to keep yourself from feeling isolated. However you choose to do it, surround yourself with life!

Shortly after Barbara lost her husband, her sister brought her a puppy to keep her company. Barbara thought her sister was crazy and told her so. She was not feeling up to the challenge of housebreaking a puppy. She was even afraid she would forget to feed the poor thing. Barbara's sister pledged her assistance in the care and feeding of her new pet but absolutely refused to take the dog back until Barbara had given the project a fair trial.

Within days Barbara began to see the wisdom in her sister's act of kindness. Because she was responsible for another living thing, especially one that was so helpless and dependent, she was forced not to dwell too much upon her loss. She continued to do her grief work, of course, but her puppy never allowed her to get too focused on herself. His presence forced Barbara to get out and walk each day, which not only brought her into contact with the beauty of nature but helped her to maintain a healthful regimen of exercise which thwarted her inclination to get depressed. Besides, his feet were too big for his body and he was unbelievably clumsy. He gave Barbara ample reasons to laugh even in the midst of her grief. Now, years later, Barbara's dog is her faithful companion and protector. She says that puppy was the most thoughtful gift her sister ever gave her.

While it is never wise to adopt a pet without considering the decision carefully, you might find that it's exactly what you need.

In the meantime, try surrounding yourself with other forms of life that may be somewhat less demanding, always remembering that Jesus said that he is the way, the truth and the life (see John 14:6). It is his life with which we most need to surround ourselves. It is the Holy Spirit whose companionship we most need to claim. Drawing closer to Christ during our time of grief will help us understand more fully what life is.

58 Acceptance

> *My frame was not hidden from you when I was made in the secret place. When I was woven together in the depths of the earth, your eyes saw my unformed body. All the days ordained for me were written in your book before one of them came to be.*
>
> **Psalm 139:15-16**

I N the days just following the loss of someone we love we often hear the word *acceptance* bandied about as if it were synonymous with Nirvana. We are told we must "accept" our loss and look to Jesus. It often seems as if people are telling us that we dare not look to Christ until we accept our loved one's death. This is sheer balderdash. We can look to the Lord even in the midst of our stormiest emotions, before we have come anywhere near the point of acceptance.

Eventually, however, we do come face-to-face with our need to accept what has happened, not so that we can finally prove that we are worthy of God's help with our grief but because we can never fully heal without it.

At first, we may interpret acceptance as being glad for our loss, but gradually we come to see that as nonsense. We don't approve of our loved one's death. We are not glad for it. We hate it with every fiber of our being.

We may also see acceptance as being synonymous with forgetting the one we have lost and "just getting on with it." That is nonsense too. None of us can forget someone we have truly loved. We would be abnormal if we could. Ray never wants to forget his father. Ray's dad conveyed important messages to him in regard to work, relationships, honesty and a whole host of other essential lessons about life. Forgetting his dad would mean figuratively amputating a part of himself. That is neither desirable nor healthful.

True acceptance comes to us when we reach a point in our grieving process when we can be absolutely certain that, although we may not understand the why of our loss, we know that our loved one's death did not take God by surprise. It did not happen because God was caught napping one day. We can be sure that all of our loved one's days were written in God's book before one of them came to be. And we will know that even the time of our loved one's death was a part of God's plan, both for his or her life and for our own.

Acceptance will also enable us to look back over our grief process, at the path of pain and the valleys of despair, and say, "Yes, Lord. I see now. You *have* used all of this to purify me, to help me grow." We are not glad for our loved one's death but, rather, we are glad for the way in which God has redeemed our grief. When we finally come to a point of acceptance, we can see that we actually needed all those painful times before our healing could be complete.

Acceptance is not a gut-wrenching attempt to look peaceful. It is a calm assurance that the person we have lost will always be with us because of the contribution that person has made to our lives. It is an acceptance of God's will for us even when his plan and ours don't match up. It is a "Yes, Lord, and amen" even when we don't get our own way. It is our final step toward healing.

59 There Is an End

> *The Lord will be your everlasting light,*
> *and your days of sorrow will end.*
>
> **Isaiah 60:20**

IN the early stages of our grief it seems as if we will never again know freedom from sorrow. We ask ourselves, "Will I ever find anything to stop my descent into this pit?" "Will this pain ever go away?" "Will I always feel as if I have just had my heart torn in two?" As countless others who have fallen into this same pit can attest, there is an end. It will not come immediately, but it will come. And we know that the less time and energy we invest in bottling up our pain and sorrow, the sooner it will come.

We are aware that if your grief is very new these words will sound immensely hollow. You may even feel that you don't want this pain to come to an end right now. Your sorrow may seem like the only thing that's keeping your loved one close to you. If that's the case, you may wish to mark this page and come back to it at some time in the future.

For others, however, these words may be timely. You may have advanced to a stage in your grieving process where you are looking for some words of hope, some promise of light at the end of the tunnel. It is for you that we say, "There is an end."

By this we do not mean that you will reach a time in your life when you will never feel a pang of regret or melancholy as you think of your loss. Most of us continue to miss our loved one to some extent, regardless of how long it has been since his or her death. But that pang of regret, that moment of melancholy, will be fleeting. Your pain will no longer pull up a chair and plan to stay awhile. The impact of the pain carried by those moments will be but a whisper.

So why is it important for you to hear that this immense aching in your heart and mind will eventually come to an end? Simply because pain seems to be more bearable if we know it will only last for a season. There will come a day, probably when you least expect it, when the dark clouds will be swept away and the sun will shine through, a time when you will feel rested at the end of a night's sleep rather than edgy and troubled, a day when the aching in your chest will cease and you will begin to breathe freely again. You will catch yourself smiling over nothing in particular. Then you will know that your long trail through the darkness is coming to an end.

In the meantime, go easy on yourself. Give yourself the time to grieve fully. There is no reason to rush. You will reach the end of this road in God's time.

60 How Long Is "Long Enough?"

There is a time for everything, and a season for every activity under heaven: a time to be born and a time to die, a time to plant and a time to uproot, a time to kill and a time to heal, a time to tear down and a time to build, a time to weep and a time to laugh, a time to mourn and a time to dance, a time to scatter stones and a time to gather them, a time to embrace and a time to refrain, a time to search and a time to give up, a time to keep and a time to throw away, a time to tear and a time to mend, a time to be silent and a time to speak, a time to love and a time to hate, a time for war and a time for peace.

Ecclesiastes 3:1-8

MOST of us feel that we can handle almost anything if we just know how long it will take. There is something comforting about knowing where to find the end. It is only natural that we should want to know how long we must grieve if we expect to do a "good job." Unfortunately, there is no ideal answer to the question, "How long is long enough?" And, whether you believe it or not, it really is a good thing that we have no answer. There is a hazard in having a reference point. We tend to turn a reference point into a finish line if we are not careful.

Still, there are some facts that may be helpful to you. Most authorities agree that we weather the toughest stages of grief during the first year after the loss of a loved one. That first year is filled with all the anniversaries and events that we have been accustomed to sharing with the one we love. Each date gives us cause to grieve again. Whether or not these dates and events seemed particularly significant during our loved one's life does not really have any bearing on our response to them now that he or she is gone. Each one brings about a fresh awareness of our loss.

Because this first year is the most difficult, however, it is also likely to be the most healing—if we allow ourselves the freedom to grieve fully and genuinely.

When we are confronted with a potentially healing situation we have the choice to participate in it or resist it. A patient who has had cardiac surgery can choose to sit back and wait for his heart to heal or he can participate in the therapy that will strengthen his heart, preventing a recurrence of the problem. The more actively he responds to his body's needs the more complete his healing.

On the other hand, he can ignore his doctor's orders and carry on as if nothing has happened. Outwardly it may not look as if he is doing anything damaging but appearances are not everything. A heart patient can kill himself with negligence if he is not careful.

The same is true for a "grief patient." By ignoring our pain and sorrow we can kill ourselves by inches, sometimes emotionally, sometimes physically, and sometimes both.

If your grief continues to be ever present beyond a year and a half, it may be appropriate to seek counseling. There may be something that is preventing you from fully healing. Perhaps you have unresolved issues to which you must attend before you can finally put the past behind you. Your pastor or a counselor can help you identify issues you may not be aware even exist.

The most important thing to remember is that every individual is different. You are the only one who can answer the question: "How long is long enough?" The only realistic answer to that question is: "As long as it takes."

61 Sufficent Grace

> But he [God] said to me, "My grace is sufficient for you, for my power is made perfect in weakness." Therefore I will boast all the more gladly about my weaknesses, so that Christ's power may rest on me. That is why, for Christ's sake, I delight in weaknesses, in insults, in hardships, in persecutions, in difficulties. For when I am weak, then I am strong.   2 Corinthians 12:9-10

MANY of us reach a stage in our grief when we begin to feel embarrassed by the fact that we are still grieving. It's as if there's an expiration date stamped somewhere on the grieving process. We begin to stuff down our tears when we hear a piece of music or see an old photograph that reminds us of the one we lost for fear of embarrassing ourselves or those around us. We tell ourselves that we don't want to make those around us uncomfortable, that we wish to spare *them*. Usually, though, the truth is that we don't want to be criticized for being weak. We sense, correctly or incorrectly, that showing our grief is some kind of *faux pas*. We fear that people are saying, "Is he (or she) *still* grieving?" We worry that they won't want to be around us anymore if we don't put our tears away soon.

How much better it is to be true to ourselves and our feelings, to be honest about our "weakness," if that's what it is. Such honesty was certainly good enough for the apostle Paul, as he expressed himself in 2 Corinthians. Of course there are those who may genuinely feel uncomfortable with our continuing grief because they see it as a plea for their continued support. We can quietly and lovingly release those people from their feeling of obligation. We can assure them that our grief is not necessarily a plea for help, it simply *is*.

We can actually turn our continuing grief into a witness for the Lord. Not a witness to the foolish notion that God will magically whisk away our grief, but to the fact that he walks with us in our grief. God is always available and his grace is sufficient. We can bear witness to God's goodness even in the midst of our sorrow. We can use this time—this sorrow—to bring us closer to God. We can choose to revel in our dependency upon the Lord as Paul did. Not in a mawkish, woe-is-me, sort of way, but in a way that will bring glory to God rather than to us and to our fortitude. We can be a living testimony to the truth contained in the words, "My grace is sufficient for you."

Today, you can determine to be true to yourself and to your feelings. Allow others to see your faith in action *through* your sorrow, not in spite of it.

62 | He Has Overcome the World

> *In this world you will have trouble. But take heart! I have overcome the world.*
>
> **John 16:33**

I N his book *Where Is God When It Hurts?* Philip Yancey says that those who heard Christ when he said the words recorded in John 16:33 must have felt immense excitement. Yet, scant hours later, those same men were overwhelmed by hopelessness. They must have felt as if Christ had been beaten by death itself. Yancey goes on to say that, for a few days, it must have seemed as if the world had overcome God.

Do you feel as if death has overcome God? Have you wondered whether God was caught napping the day your loved one died? You wouldn't be the first. For many years Lynn struggled with confusion and resentment toward God over the loss of her child. She kept wondering whether God was responsible. If so, was it proof that God just didn't care or did it prove that he was powerless to prevent her loss?

Eventually, Lynn realized that rather than asking, "Is God responsible?" she needed to ask, "How can I respond to this so that it produces *perseverance, character and hope?*" (Romans 5:4).

We are aware that that question may sound awfully hollow to you right now. Your grief may be too fresh for you to feel like asking God to use your suffering to produce those character traits. If so, don't despair. God is patient with his children.

Regardless of the way you feel right now, it can be helpful to know that it's possible for all this pain to be redeemed by God, to know that he can turn this pain into something useful, something from which you can learn—if not today, then sometime in the future.

Unfortunately, most Christians in this country seem to have the idea that suffering is always to be avoided. If we are suffering then either we are being punished for something or our faith is being tested. Either way, most of us want it to *stop*. On the other hand, the Scriptures paint a different picture of suffering. There are many references to suffering as a means of purification and of sharing fellowship with Christ. Does that sound like a callous thing to say to someone who is grieving? Perhaps. But it only seems callous so long as we are looking at *this* life. When we take the long view, when we realize that this pain—this life—is but a single moment in the scope of eternity, it does not seem so anymore. Suddenly, it seems more like a life-saving truth that needs to be shouted from the housetops.

We can say with all faith and hope that we "consider that our present sufferings are not worth comparing with the glory that will be revealed in us" (Romans 8:18). We can truthfully and joyfully shout that this pain is insignificant in light of the fact that we "are being transformed into his likeness with ever-increasing glory, which comes from the Lord, who is the Spirit" (2 Corinthians 3:18).

63 We Are Like Grass

Lord, help me to realize how brief my time on earth will be. Help me to know that I am here for but a moment more. We are like grass that is green in the morning but mowed down and withered before the evening shadows fall. Teach us to number our days and recognize how few they are; help us to spend them as we should.

Psalms 39:4; 90:5, 12 (TLB)

SOONER or later during our grieving process we begin to wonder what purpose there is in all this pain. When we finally see our private storm of grief begin to clear we tend to look around, assessing the changes in the landscape of our lives. It is only natural. Our sense of the order and purpose in God's creation leads us to believe that at least some of the changes will be beneficial ones. It's important to understand at that moment that while there are many lessons we can learn from our experience, God leaves it up to us to claim them. One lesson we can learn is the one the Psalmist asked God to teach us. "Teach us to number our days... help us to spend them as we should."

Those of us who have been touched by death are particularly aware of the brevity of our days here on earth. We are especially motivated to spend what days God has given us in ways that are pleasing to him. We have seen death's outcome. We can allow that sight to frighten and paralyze us, or we can allow it to activate and inspire us to change our lives and our lifestyle. We, more than those who have not been touched by death, are aware of the preciousness of our relationships. We see more clearly the value of each and every moment.

Lynn knew a woman whose life was transformed by her mother's death. She went from being a complaining, judgmental person to a woman at peace with her Lord and her family. Death forced her to look at the pettiness of her value system. To her credit, she was courageous enough to discard it and find a God-inspired value system to take its place.

Many of us do not need to make such sweeping changes in our lives but nearly all of us make some pretty astounding discoveries about ourselves and the nature of life during our grieving process. Perhaps we have learned that we need to take a long, hard look at our priorities. Maybe that next promotion and all the overtime it will entail isn't really as important as we thought. Or the time we spend pursuing that perfectly spotless house or perfectly polished car could be better spent on other things. Perhaps we learn that our emotions—even intense ones—although uncomfortable, will not kill us as we once thought. We learn that we can be vulnerable and real and live to tell about it. Whatever lessons we learn, we must resolve to prevent them from being stolen from us by time and circumstance.

Take some time today to write down some of the lessons this period of grief has taught you. Continue to write down new lessons as you recognize them in the days and weeks ahead.

64 | Clinging to the Pain

Still, there's no denying that in some sense I "feel better," and with that comes at once a sort of shame, and a feeling that one is under a sort of obligation to cherish and foment and prolong one's unhappiness.

C.S. Lewis
A Grief Observed

*I*N the beginning of our grief we may often have asked God to relieve us of the crushing, unending ache in our hearts. We may have made bargains with God, asking him to give us a respite from the grief, if only for a few moments. At times, we may have felt as if it was going to kill us. After a while, however, we become rather accustomed to that ache in our middle. It almost takes on the familiarity of a friend. It becomes a constant in a universe that has declined into chaos. Our pain has not necessarily diminished. It isn't even less significant than it was before. It's just familiar.

There are those who will scornfully dismiss that

notion but it has been known to happen. In fact, it happens more often than most of us would like to think. We are created in the image of the One who makes order out of chaos. We naturally seek order. We enjoy predictability. There is security in the familiar. It is not so far-fetched to believe that we can become hooked on the security of our grief. We have structured our lives around it for some time. We do not willfully choose to base our existence on the order provided by our pain, but it is one way to cope with it.

Then one day we wake up and realize that the ache within has diminished and we may wonder what has gone wrong. We may worry that we have somehow entered a state of denial that is depriving us of the pain that has become so much a part of our lives. When that happens we are at loose ends for a time, unable to walk without stumbling. Only now we are not stumbling over our pain. We are stumbling because we are accustomed to compensating for the load we have been carrying, a load that is now absent, or at least diminished. Life seems a little strange without it.

A new life, born of healing and acceptance, means change. It creates a new order, not all at once, but gradually. In the meantime, we are in a state of transition, which isn't always comfortable. It can even be a little frightening.

We may worry, too, that our lack of pain means that we have forgotten how precious our loved one was. We may have decided, somewhere deep inside, that our pain is a tribute to our loved one and without that pain we are not memorializing him or her suitably. We may worry that others will think us cold and unfeeling when we move ahead with our lives, that people will think we have stopped loving the one we have lost.

It is best to face these fears head-on, to acknowledge that our pain has become familiar and that we are a little bit frightened of what life will hold without it. If that's true, it doesn't mean that we are hopelessly "sick." We are simply human. We must remind ourselves, sometimes sternly, that while there is nothing wrong with predictability and security, it can stand in the way of our continued growth and healing. We know that God has walked with us through the storm. We can trust him to walk with us, just as faithfully, through the change that follows the storm.

65 Reaching Out

Praise be to the God and Father of our Lord Jesus Christ, the Father of compassion and the God of all comfort, who comforts us in all our troubles, so that we can comfort those in any trouble with the comfort we ourselves have received from God.

2 Corinthians 1:3-4

THERE comes a time in our grief process when we need to take action in order to continue healing. We need to look life—or death—squarely in the eye and profess that we are not helpless victims, even in the face of great loss. Psychologists call it "taking your power back." Christians might prefer to call it reaffirming God's power in our lives.

There are nearly as many ways to reaffirm God's power in our lives as there are people who wish to. Couples who have lost a child to crib death may choose to begin a local extension of the support group for other parents grieving the loss of children through

SIDS. Mothers Against Drunk Driving (MADD) was formed by two women who had lost children in traffic accidents caused by drunk drivers. The support group called Parents of Murdered Children was formed by people whose pain was like no other they had ever imagined. Others who were recovering from grief and loss have chosen to become involved in hospice work and grief counseling. Ray chose to become a psychologist in order to assist people as they traveled through their grief process. Lynn became a counselor and makes an effort to call or visit women from her church who have suffered losses similar to her own. The list of possibilities is almost endless. What we do is not nearly as important as the fact that we do it. Comforting others with the same comfort you yourself have received from God will help you to heal also.

If you are still in the early stages of your grief you will want to postpone, for a while longer, getting involved in any kind of outreach. It is best not to overload yourself or to short-circuit your grief by concentrating on others' needs before it's time. But, if you are beginning to get an "itch" to *do* something, if your ears perk up when you hear that someone else has just lost a loved one and you wonder what you can do to help, then perhaps it's time to begin to reach out to those who are just beginning their journey down the road of grief. Pray about it. Ask God whether it is time. Then ask where he would have you spend your energies. The rewards will be great and your healing will be multiplied.

66 Walking through the Fire

Fear not, for I have redeemed you; I have summoned you by name; you are mine. When you pass through the waters, I will be with you; and when you pass through the rivers, they will not sweep over you. When you walk through the fire, you will not be burned; the flames will not set you ablaze. For I am the Lord, your God, the Holy One of Israel, your Savior.

Isaiah 43:1-3

WHEN we lose someone we love, it is possible for us to keep our wound open until the day we join our loved one in death. One way to keep our wound open is by ignoring our pain, refusing to remain true to our grief process. It is also possible, however, to keep prodding our wound, preventing it from fully healing. We can dwell too much upon our sorrow, shielding ourselves from the reasons God gives us to rejoice.

Grief has a bittersweet quality to it. Personal pain

can be exquisitely beautiful in its own way. Those statements may sound awful but they are nonetheless true. Creative, artistic people, in particular, have been known to be seduced by the beauty of their pain, treasuring it rather than pursuing healing. Grief has a way of compelling an artist to create. A creative urge is often fueled, or at least complemented, by pain and sorrow. Many of the world's most splendid paintings were created by artists who were in the midst of emotional pain. Some of the world's most magnificent music and poetry was drafted by composers or writers who were suffering, either emotionally or physically. It can be terribly tempting to remain in our pain in order to fuel our creativity. But that is not what God has in mind for his people. He has called us by name and we are his. It is not up to us to repudiate his claim on us in order to remain at the peak of our creativity. He intends for us to grow and heal. It is not part of his plan for us to remain in the deep waters of sorrow, to be consumed by the flames of our pain. He wants us to go through the waters, unhurt. He wants us to walk through the flames, unburned.

This can create a dilemma for an artist. What can we use to fuel our creativity once we are free from pain and sorrow? God's Word supplies us with the answer. We can take onto ourselves God's burden for the hurting masses of the world. We can remain in the Scriptures and in prayer to such an extent that we feel Christ's pain when we witness the heartaches of his people, when we observe the vast numbers of people who do not know him.

When we train ourselves to claim Christ's burden for humankind we will find ample opportunities to create beautiful masterpieces that attest to the truth. We can paint or draw magnificent depictions of humanity's need for Christ. We can write superb poetry that points the way to Christ, that attests to the healing available in and through him. We can compose songs that call God's people to repentance, songs that confirm God's goodness and lovingkindness. We can stand in awe as God elevates our creativity to a new level. We can make our lives—and our pain—count for the kingdom of God. We will discover as we do these things that claiming Christ's burden, sharing Christ's pain, carries with it none of the ill effects on our physical health and emotional well-being that nursing our private grief carries with it.

If you have been concerned, as many artists are, that you will lose some of your creative "edge" once your grief has run its course, take your concerns to the Lord in prayer. Ask God to give you a burden for his people. Ask Christ to give you an intimate understanding of his heart for his people. Then, pursue your personal healing without fear. And be prepared to exceed your perceived potential as an artist.

67 | *Blessed Assurance*

Now it is God who... has given us the Spirit as a deposit, guaranteeing what is to come. **2 Corinthians 5:5**

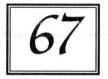WHILE loving concern and empathy are welcome and necessary for the Christian who is grieving, in the final analysis, these things are stop-gap measures for handling grief if they are not hemmed in on all sides by the message of the Scriptures. Certainly, we need fellow believers to help us bear our grief, but there is only One who can help us grow in and through our grief, only One who has the power to heal the wound resulting from our loss.

Once we have passed the initial stages of our grief and we are able to think clearly enough to pray and read the Bible, we need to make the Scriptures our resting place and the Lord our sounding board, not exclusively—we are still designed to fellowship with others of our kind—but consistently. The Scriptures are full of comforting news for those who have suffered loss. Our grief is still real, of course, but we need not grieve as those who have no hope. We have hope that's based on the reality of the resurrection. We have the Holy Spirit within us, which is a present day assurance of our future in eternity (2 Corinthians 5:5). We have the assurance that we "shall never perish" (John 10:28). We will meet our loved ones "in the clouds" on the day of redemption.

Undeniably, we have sorrow, but not despair. We have loneliness, but we are not alone because we have the reality of Christ's presence. There are hundreds of verses of Scripture written by those who were suffering great sorrow and affliction, yet they were hopeful. Those writers who lived before us have proven God to be all that he claims to be. God is faithful and true, "an ever-present help in trouble" (Psalm 46:1).

Turn to God in this time of trouble and find yourself saying, along with the Psalmist, "How sweet are your words to my taste, sweeter than honey to my mouth!" (Psalm 119:103).

68 Not a Hill but a Spiral

> *He [God] has sent me [Christ] to bind up the brokenhearted... to comfort all who mourn, and provide for those who grieve... to bestow on them a crown of beauty instead of ashes, the oil of gladness instead of mourning, and a garment of praise instead of a spirit of despair.* Isaiah 61:1-3

MANY years ago Ray sat looking out across Detour Passage, an active shipping lane on the eastern side of Michigan's Upper Peninsula. It was dark and a gale was raging down through the narrow passage, yet he sat on the shore, oblivious to the storm. The entire world seemed to be suspended in time. Tears streamed down Ray's face. It didn't really matter that he had successfully shepherded a canoe full of terrified fathers and sons across the raging passage that day, narrowly missing being crushed against multi-million ton freighters on one side and huge boulders on the other. Nothing mattered just then. Ray was face-to-face once again with his grief over his father's death. Earlier that day, as he watched the fathers carry their sons out of the water, he had felt a stab of pain. He dunked his head in the icy water to hide his tears. Now that the nightly campfire was over, Ray had moved silently away from the group so that he could be alone.

Ray was ashamed that his feelings were so out of control. It had been six years since his father's death. Shouldn't this be over by now? Yet his pain and emptiness were undeniable. The old wounds seemed to be freshly opened. Ray struggled against his need to face his grief once more. He walked the shore as he wept and shouted at God, the sounds of the storm drowning out his words.

We process our grief in cycles. It is impossible to say with any seriousness, "There now, that's over. I'm done with my grief." We don't ascend the hill of sorrow and blithely descend the other side, never to feel another twinge of grief again. Our ascent is more of a spiral. We continually circle around and face the pain again from a slightly different vantage point. It is true, however, that if we face it courageously we will never have to face it in quite that way again.

It's wise for us to expect to deal with our loss again and again throughout life, although each time we face it, it will be less painful. Each time we face it the experience will be followed with a greater sense of wholeness and peace. But face it we will, time and time again.

As ancient sailors chose the North Star to guide them in their journeys, we can be helped immensely as we sail through this storm, if we choose as our reference point the Lord Jesus Christ. If we keep our eyes on our "north star" rather than the variable waves of our grief we will be better able to navigate the storm. We can allow Christ to comfort us, to give us a crown of beauty instead of ashes, anoint us with the oil of gladness instead of mourning, and give us a garment of praise to replace our spirit of despair. We do that by resolving to learn to know Christ better, by studying what the Scriptures tell us about who he is so that we can strive to claim his nature for our own.

Today, beginning right now, pray that God will give you a personal knowledge of Christ's power, his sufferings and himself. Ask God to nurture within you a desire to know Christ that outweighs every other desire. Before long, your view of the Bright and Morning Star will outshine all of your other concerns, including your grief.

69 The Healing Power of Time

> *For I am convinced that neither death nor life, neither angels nor demons, neither the present nor the future, nor any powers, neither height nor depth, nor anything else in all creation, will be able to separate us from the love of God that is in Christ Jesus our Lord.* Romans 8:38-39

NOT long ago Lynn decided to reread the pages of her journal, written during the time she was finally dealing with the loss of her baby. She was bowled over by the intensity of the pain reflected on those pages. She found it incomprehensible that she had actually lived through that kind of pain.

Lynn felt greatly encouraged by the incident. Her pain had faded to such a pale shade of its former depth that, until she read those pages, she literally could not remember ever having felt her sorrow with such intensity. Even after reading her journal she found that, while she was moved by the words on the page, it was as if she were reading about someone else. The pain was no longer hers to claim. We suspect that is probably true for most people. Time really is a great healer, once we have dealt adequately with our immense sorrow.

You see, during the years Lynn was using mental trickery to avoid dealing with her pain, it lost none of its intensity. It dogged her every step. It inserted itself into all of her relationships, every one of her decisions, although she was not consciously aware of it. Once she had genuinely allowed herself to grieve, her pain dissipated. We can think of no greater argument in favor of dealing forthrightly with one's grief in the first place.

Many others have the same story to tell. When their grief is new, their pain is unimaginable. It really does feel as if their anguish is going to kill them. Then, the pain fades to a shadow of what it was. It doesn't happen all at once, but it does happen—a little at a time. Time and honest grieving seem to be the keys.

Have you been avoiding your pain for a long time? Are you avoiding it now? Are you striving to keep yourself busy so that you do not have to think about it, so that there is no time or energy left within you to dwell on your immense loss? Dealing with grief can seem an intimidating task. It may even feel as if God's love will not have the power to reach you as you travel through the valley of grief that's ahead of you. Let us encourage you to face it with the help and hope available through Jesus Christ. Nothing can separate you from the love of God. He *will* walk with you through that valley, just as he did Lynn and Ray and thousands of others who can now look back on their pain as merely an element of their past. It *can* happen for you too. It will be difficult, it will be painful, but it will be so worthwhile.

70 The Christian's Perspective

> *After the resurrection the apostles never used the word death to express the close of a Christian's earthly life. They referred to the passing of a Christian as "at home with the Lord," "to depart and be with Christian," "to sleep in Jesus."*
>
> John M. Drescher
> "In Grief's Lone Hour"

As Christians we have the unique opportunity to turn even our mourning into a time of rejoicing. Only Christians have the absolute assurance that we will see our loved ones again one day. Only we have reason to rejoice even as we grieve. We would be mistaken to think that joy and sorrow are mutually exclusive. They are not. Humans have the wondrous ability to experience two seemingly opposite emotions at the same time. We have the ability to feel anger and gratefulness; we may be confused, yet full of hope and assurance, joyful in the midst of sorrow. Lynn will always be angry with

Satan for having robbed her of the experience of raising her first daughter, yet grateful for the fact that she will one day hold her in heaven. Ray will always be sad about being deprived of his father's presence during his teens, yet joyful at the thought that he, too, will see his dad on the day he joins him in the clouds along with Jesus.

Lynn's friend, Sandy, gives this wonderful illustration of the truth in regard to death. "Once, while attending a friend's funeral I sensed an awesome irony. The beautiful flowers looked alive and vibrant but, because they were cut flowers, they were actually dead. They just had the appearance of life. On the other hand, because my friend was a Christian, she was very much alive, although she had the appearance of death."

So it is with all of life. Appearances can be deceiving. Those who are without Christ may interpret our sorrow as hopelessness because they themselves would be without hope if they found themselves in a similar circumstance. Yet, our sadness, our anger, even our denial, are actually manifestations of our faith and God's goodness. God gives us our denial to shield us from the full force of our grief when we are least able to withstand it. Our freedom to be openly angry and sorrowful are reflections of our assurance that nothing we do or feel can separate us from God's love. Of all people, we are most blessed, because we have a "Daddy-God" who holds us in his arms and comforts us as his little children.

If you've reached a time in your grieving process when you are able to feel both your sadness and the joy that is rightfully yours, do not hesitate to give voice to both. If those around you find it confusing, use their confusion as an opportunity to tell them about the hope we have in and through Christ Jesus. We serve a resurrected Lord who will, indeed, meet us one day in the clouds.

"How great is the love the Father has lavished on us, that we should be called children of God!" (1 John 3:1).